TRESPASSERS WILL BE
BAPTIZED

TRESPASSERS WILL BE
BAPTIZED

THE UNORDAINED MEMOIR OF A
PREACHER'S DAUGHTER

ELIZABETH EMERSON HANCOCK

CENTER
STREET

NEW YORK BOSTON NASHVILLE

TEACH YOUR CHILDREN
© 1970 Nash Notes. All rights administered by Sony/ATV Music
Publishing, 8 Music Square West, Nashville, TN 37203.
All rights reserved. Used by permission.

Center Street
Hachette Book Group USA
237 Park Avenue
New York, NY 10017

Visit our Web site at www.centerstreet.com.

Center Street is a division of Hachette Book Group USA, Inc.
The Center Street name and logo are trademarks of Hachette Book Group
USA, Inc.

Printed in the United States of America

First Edition: June 2008
10 9 8 7 6 5 4 3 2 1

Library of Congress Cataloging-in-Publication Data
Hancock, Elizabeth Emerson.
    Trespassers will be baptized : the unordained memoir of a preacher's
daughter / Elizabeth Emerson Hancock.
        p. cm.
    ISBN-13: 978-1-59995-708-1
    ISBN-10: 1-59995-708-6
    1. Hancock, Elizabeth Emerson—Childhood and youth.
2. Children of clergy—Kentucky—Biography.
3. Baptists—Kentucky—Biography.   I. Title.
    BX6495.H265A3 2008
    286'.1092—dc22
    [B]
                            2007031643

For Dad, Mom, and Meg.
Preach on.

ACKNOWLEDGMENTS

Getting this book ready for publication was a bit like pulling the lead Christmas pageant angel off the church playground, muddy and ornery, minutes before her show, and making her into something remotely praiseworthy.

To Chris Min Park and Sarah Sper, backed by the wonderful team at Center Street, who were every inch the inspirational backstage mommas for this work. Thank you for the careful grooming, the occasional hair-pulling, and for coaxing my voice out of me without breaking a smile.

To Byrd Leavell, the Job of literary agents, who is aptly named for giving me, and so many others, wings. John 20:29.

To my family, who taught me the art of trespassing and forgiveness, and without whom there are no stories. Whoever first said that there is power in the blood didn't know the half of it.

To Mr. Munson and my junior year advanced placement English class, where this memoir was first conceived as a short personal narrative, and for the teacher who showed us our own small-town experiences could have impacts of biblical proportion.

Every little angel needs a halo, but in this case that belongs to my wonderful husband, Sean. Without his ethereal patience and strength, my heart would never have made it into print.

And finally, to all those who ever trespassed against me. You may or may not know who you are, but Jesus does. Wink and Amen to that.

CONTENTS

AUTHOR'S NOTE

This work is a point of view, recalled through the great stained glass of time and memory. Such points of view are as varied and unique as religious experiences themselves. My intent in writing this book was not to defame or devalue any person, church, or faith. Names and characteristics of individuals have been changed or composited, and certain events have been altered, compressed, and presented out of sequence to protect the integrity and privacy of the believers, and of the belief acts, portrayed in this book.

But the fruit of the Spirit is love, joy, peace,
patience, kindness, goodness, faithfulness,
gentleness, and self-control.

—Galatians 5:22–23. The legendary "Fruits of
the Spirit" Bible verse, and the theme of three-
quarters of the Vacation Bible Schools I ever attended. The Southern Baptists who raised me
were not always known for being original. The
same could not be said for the ways in which I
learned my lessons.

One of our yard sales

Invocation

In east-central Kentucky, where I grew up, yard sales were spiritual affairs. People laid the holiest parts of their pasts on the altar: china patterns in small, paltry sets, for which incompleteness was a mark of shame (the marriage clearly hadn't lasted long enough for the set to be finished); self-help books (not deemed subversive until after they'd spent at least two weeks on the best-seller list); wine and cordial sets (reason for purging them: self-explanatory).

On the first Saturday in July 1982, when my grandmother Mimi's new street held its annual Public Cleansing of the

Sinful, the Embarrassing, the Tacky, and the Used-Up (officially known as the Town-Wide Community Yard Sale), Momma and Aunt Kit turned Mimi's front yard into a veritable mecca of the Bluegrass. Their own daddy had passed away some ten years before, and Mimi had finally remarried. Her new husband's house was smaller, so lots of old had to pass away, for pennies on the dollar, before the new could come.

My sister, cousins, and I sat on the edge of the driveway, in awe of Momma and Kit. Wearing their signature yard sale day uniforms—Bermudas over bathing suits and halos of giant aluminum rollers—they gave off an aura that made piles of warped Tupperware seem magnetic. No other yard on the block was doing as much business. But it wasn't our mothers' entrepreneurship that had us concerned.

All up and down the block, kids our age were cashing in on the yard sales, too. Each time a grown-up entered a driveway, she had to practically trip over a teetering, scrap-wood refreshment "stand" staffed by some barefoot child who looked like a pitiful, melting toad out in the sun. A pitiful, melting, *moneymaking* little toad. My sister and I knew we could do better.

Meg and I took a few of Mimi's empty moving cartons from the garage and set to work on our own stand. We set it up right at the driveway's edge—almost in the road—where it couldn't be missed. And sure enough, no one passing by missed a glance at what we were offering, spelled out in blood-red tempera paint:

Baptisms: 25 Cents.

And below it, in tiny print:

But if you do not have any money, it is free.

2

Lesson 1

Meg and me (I'm wearing a Guess jeans skirt Aunt Kit gave me)

Kindness

ACID-WASHED SAMARITANS

For a true Kentucky girl, it is possible to baptize out the sin, but not the Blue. And for that reason, no worse punishment can be devised for her than imprisonment in a televisionless guest bedroom in the middle of March Madness.

Cold-turkey withdrawal from basketball is the most cruel and unusual penance that can be inflicted upon anyone in the Bluegrass. Age doesn't matter, we're all like those crack-cocaine babies—addicted from the first jump ball. In fact, when I was a kid, Wildcat basketball was the only such addiction respected—no, *encouraged*—by the Southern Baptist Church, where being in attendance at services was held in greater esteem than being in God's graces. If your house burned to the ground on a Saturday, well, you'd better get your rear end in the pew on Sunday morning and thank the Lord for sparing your life. Your wife died? Sorry, but you'd best show up immediately and let the Women's League fuss over you, or else they'd take offense.

But if it was Sunday and the Game was on, well, that was different. God made the Wildcats, and the Wildcats glorified Him through their goal-shattering, soul-shattering play. If your church held a Kentucky Wildcat basketball player—current *or* former—on its membership roll, and you managed to secure his autographed jersey for your trophy case (typically signed with the citation to the athlete's favorite Bible verse), then you had officially acquired the Holy Grail of missions tools. Who *knew* how many stadiumfuls of souls that jersey might draw to the Lord's side?

And yet my mother refused to respect the almighty force of Kentucky Basketball. It was for that reason that I silently prayed for her soul, even as I wrote in my Bible notebook and cursed her name during that one afternoon of cruelest isolation. I was almost nine years old and I was in trouble. But more than that, I was worried. I really hoped God would forgive my mother for making me miss the game.

It only made me madder when I saw my little sister, out like a light on the guest twin bed next to mine. This was the one talent that always made me jealous of Meg—she could escape into sleep from anything, anytime, anywhere, and it took her less than a minute. A punishment like the guest-room prison didn't have to be a punishment for her. She didn't have to endure the slow burn of sunlight lowering slat-by-slat through the mini blinds and rusty bike wheels going on a last ride for the evening. Most maddening of all, she didn't have to trudge through some dumb paperback from the preteen section of the Tucker's Mill Elementary library (hand-chosen by Momma, who taught sixth grade at the time).

I hated preteen books. As I noted in my Bible notebook, if Jesus could read one, He would proclaim that "thou art the most asinine things ever written." They certainly weren't made for girls like me who understood the meaning of *asinine* (which was taught to me by my father, by way of one of his sermons). All the girls in those books knew how to do was sit around and whine about how ugly and fat they were and how nobody liked them. I had the good sense to know that I was beautiful even without a bra (and in the church, I was even holy-royal). Still, were I to grow up to be such a whiner, Momma would have no one but herself and Judy Blume to thank.

So, partly out of frustration with *Ramona Forever*, and partly because I was tired of taking my punishment alone, I threw the book against the far wall, right above Meg's head. With a groan, she half opened one eye. Her round face was puffy with sleep and red on one side; the word SHEPHERD from the embroidery on her pillowcase had embedded itself into her cheek.

"You woke me up, you . . . you . . . booger!" Meg shouted, still drugged in sleep. (I made note of the hesitation in her speech, the self-correction her bleary mind had made before she settled on what put-down name she was going to call me. This was a cautious, practiced art in Baptist childhood—would-be "cursing" had to be manipulated so that it wouldn't burn Jesus's ears, but would still offend your target to the maximum extent possible. Meg had mostly learned the art from our neighbor kid Joey Stinson, a true master. Just weeks before she and I landed in that guest room, Meg had come home in frantic tears from the Stinsons' backyard. She'd finally admitted, after Momma calmed her down, that "Joey called me a mitch!")

I was usually ready to counter *booger* with something related to diarrhea (putting my holy dignity aside by necessity, in emergency circumstances), but I knew that in this case, starting a fight might result in an extended sentence. If we could just stay quiet—*please, Lord*—we might be released in time to see the last quarter of the game.

"You know what's a worse name than *booger*?" I asked, eyes wide as I could make them. "*Beazus*. A girl in that book Momma made me read is really named Beazus. Can you believe that? I don't know if her parents are crazy Pentecostals or what."

It worked. Meg fell back on the bed and laughed. Thank goodness she was only six, and I had two and a half years of cleverness on her.

Normally, Meg never joked about names. She thought her own first name, Margaret, was an old-lady name, and she was correct. My mother and father named us Elizabeth and Margaret because they wanted us to sound dignified when we were older. Momma always told us it was our Christian duty to live up to those names. And on that March Sunday in 1986, I was convinced I was doing a good job of that, despite the misunderstandings of my elders. *Elizabeth* was the name of the most dignified movie star ever to walk the earth, and I was convinced I was following in her footsteps. True, my parents couldn't afford to make me one of the Kentucky "horse kids," so any hopes of *National Velvet II* were out of the question. But to my credit, I took ballet and could do one-handed cartwheels, and my mother painted my nails with real woman's polish (not the kiddy Tinkerbell brand that Meg could drink without dying).

I was certain it was only by God's graces that Meg still had years of growing up to do, because as a six-year-old Meg was *not* dignified. Ever since the first traces of spring warmth appeared that March, she'd taken to wearing an old pair of our neighbor Teddy Frank's swimming trunks as regular shorts. She just wore them day after day until Sunday morning, when Momma had to take them off with Meg kicking and screaming. Often I wondered just how the same sanctified, holy-born DNA could flow through her veins as mine.

But once in a great while, Meg had a thought of pure theological genius. And there in the guest room, in our darkest hour of faith, one of those inspired questions hit her:

"If Jesus is going to punish us anyway, why does Momma get to do it, too?" Meg asked. She walked her feet up the wall and picked her nose—the yogi-style meditative pose of the Christian child of the South.

"I don't know," I told her. "I think it's because she knows He really *won't* do anything to us, because He *knows* we weren't wrong. But I prayed to Him that I was sorry, just in case."

"Me, too. But I was falling asleep and I don't know if I got it in in time to count."

I turned over and stared out the window, out to the sidewalk where the Stinson kids were coming home from the new indoor pool at the Catholic rec center. Mrs. Stinson had a popped pool float in one hand and was dragging one of her kids by the other. The kid was squalling up a storm, rubbing a rear end that had been recently slapped. I let out a little giggle, the kind you always giggled as a child whenever you saw another child get spanked in public. You didn't know where such a laugh came from or what ungodly force put it there at that time, but it came up anyway like a big embarrassing burp and was tough to swallow back.

I stared at that poor, persecuted Stinson child, and I thought about how Momma had dragged me home by the arm like that, just that morning. I thought about how I would have preferred a spanking to the jail sentence. I thought, deep in that still-undeveloped part of my little heart that was born to question older people, about whether or not I deserved punishment at all. For as my Bible notebook would proclaim, and as I would tell the Lord face-to-face if I had the chance, Mrs. Mounts was the one who really started it.

Mrs. Joetta Mounts had taken over teaching both my Sunday School class and my GA group in January. GA stands for "Girls in Action," and in the Southern Baptist Church it can best be described as Girl Scouts Gone Holy. A girl was eligible to start attending GA troop meetings when she began the first grade. The goal of the program was to instill the Southern Baptist Convention's focus on world missions in the population of six-year-old girls, and let them grow in Christ's charity from there. We earned a badge for each level of missions study we completed, up through the sixth grade, and these were displayed on a pageant-style sash worn each year at a recognition program. When a girl became a teenager, she was eligible to promote into the Acteens program (Eagle Scouts at the Seraphim Level). You did not get cookies to sell in the GAs, but one year I remember sampling the putrid porridge of the pagan Shuma-something tribe of Liberia.

The Mounts GA group met in a little room in the back of the church that had a crooked rainbow painted on the wall, and a scary-looking Noah with a great big head and feet that looked like mashed potatoes. Week after week, we sat there and listened to fat Mrs. Mounts tell us how much we were helping the missions effort when we dressed up like Ethiopians and sang in front of the church. I felt like I was lying when I nodded, as if I believed Mrs. Mounts, but to question what she said aloud might be sassing, and I didn't know which was the worse sin, lying or back talk. (When there were two sins at once, though, I thought it was written in the Word that the older person got to pick which one counted, so I didn't talk back.)

At the time, Meg was not really old enough to be in GAs. She had an off-birthday and was too young to be in the big-girl class by a weekend, but she was too old to be put in the baby nursery. Mrs. Mounts just let her sit and color at first, but she took the coloring book away when Meg started giving all the Bible people red eyes. (Meg wasn't that old at the time, but she was smart enough to make the connection between superpowers and laser eyes. If the Lord could turn water into wine, by gosh, Meg knew He was entitled to laser eyes, too, and she aimed to give them to Him.) But after the coloring book was snatched, Meg just had to sit and be quiet like the rest of us.

She still managed the occasional brush with holy-superheroism, mostly when prayer circle time rolled around. Prayer circle always turned into sort of a contest by the end, where everyone competed to see who was in most need of divine help. Someone would start the bidding by asking for prayers for their momma's bad headaches or their grandpa's arthritis—a solid effort, but worth only a "that's too bad" from Mrs. Mounts, at most. Someone else usually one-upped this by asking for prayers for their teenage cousin who got drunk on Saturday night—again, a good effort, and sometimes rewarded by Mrs. Mounts making notes in her own personal prayer booklet, which looked a little like a meter maid's notepad. It was then, when all eyes searched the room for a last-minute sniper of a bid, that Meg would make her move, simply and matter-of-factly: "Our Mimi is in a *coma*. That means she is part alive and sick and part dead." It always came out sounding like a plea and a challenge rolled into one. *And just how are you going to pray away that combo, lady?* Mrs. Mounts never had an answer. Neither did any of our Sunday School teachers, or Daddy for that matter, when I'd ask him directly how we could force God's hand in the matter. He said that we just had to pray about it. That that was what Great and Almighty Prayer was for. When he said this, it made me think of prayer as something more like a limp-wristed weakling, without laser eyes, and without even the upper-body strength to lift my feeble grandmother on into heaven. It scared me a little to think that this was my father's hero.

The GA term ran from January to March, during the second half of Sunday services. At that last meeting of the year, that morning, Mrs. Mounts had promised us a movie and treats.

Now, anyone who ever attended church as a child knows that any treat you were promised by a church leader would inevitably be a big disappointment. That is, unless you were a kid from the Shawneetown Mission next door and you only had rocks to play with. And if you felt even a teensy bit let down inside when you got the treat, you were supposed to feel ashamed for not being grateful that you were *not* a Shawneetown kid with only rocks to play with.

Take Mrs. Mounts's movie, for example. Right as I laid myself flat-out on the cool classroom linoleum and watched her start to fumble with the VCR, I prayed with all my heart that it would be *E.T.* Deep down, though, I knew I had to prepare fake joy for the grainy David and Goliath cartoon it would, and did, turn out to be. And Lord, even though I knew being ungrateful was a sin, I just couldn't repent fast enough for that treat. It was what it always was—purple-colored water with no sugar and a cup of peanuts with no salt.

Like I said, I had no call to be surprised. My father has always maintained that the treats Southern Baptists give out at church are tied right to the heart of the religion. And the religion, he says, is all about trapdoors.

"There are people in our church who think the earth is covered in trapdoors," he told me once after a particularly heart-wrenching choir party in which we were actually given milk and slices of wheat bread, "and each of those doors is baited with the sweetest things in life. They think once you reach out and try to take those good things off the door, Satan pushes a button somewhere and you go straight to the bottom."

"So Mrs. Mounts thinks there are trapdoors in the Sunday School room?" I asked him.

"Mrs. Mounts thinks that if she puts sugar in your Kool-Aid, in two weeks you'll be on crack cocaine."

"But can't people just take the good thing off the trap-door when they see it," I wondered, "and not just stand there on it and wait to fall?"

"Well, no," he said. "The Southern Baptist philosophy rests largely on the principle that all God's glorious, perfect children are also dumb as dirt."

Lying there on that church room floor, with the little brown flecks in the linoleum that made the tiles look like vomit, I thought about how dumb as dirt Mrs. Mounts's cartoon movie was. But then, like a miracle, the real Savior intervened. It amazed me that a blessing could be disguised as Meg. She had been sawing logs over in the corner since the birth of David, and suddenly she was whispering in my ear.

"I have a stomachache, Sissy. I'm not making it up, I promise."

I noticed that Meg had little flecks of crayon wax pressed into her cheek, where it had lain against the floor.

"Okay, let's go." I sighed, pretending it was a chore to take her to the bathroom, because it usually was. Momma would never let us go to the bathroom alone, and sometimes, in restaurants, Meg would work herself into having to go just to see what the inside of a different bathroom looked like. That day, though, I was secretly relieved to get out of Mrs. Mounts's "treat" of a movie.

We walked up to Mrs. Mounts, who was asleep herself in a big rocking chair. I could see the reflection of the movie dancing across her big, frog-eyed glasses. The armbands of her short-sleeved knit shirt were squeezing the fat on the tops of her arms so tight that it looked painful. I wondered how she stayed asleep for the squeezing, but for some reason I was afraid to reach out and wake her up. Meg was not.

"Good Lord!" Mrs. Mounts jumped, forgetting that she had said *Good Lord*. "I am afraid you caught me resting my eyes."

"Meg has a tummyache. Can I take her, ma'am?" I said as charmingly as possible. Mrs. Mounts just nodded and turned back to the movie, as if she was worried she might have missed something important.

We tiptoed out the door in our sock feet and then broke into a run as soon as we were in the mile-long hallway, and not just because Meg had to go. Something about a church hallway when no one was there to watch, shush, or boss us made it the free-est-feeling place in the world.

Meg ran into the stall and left the door standing open, and

I flopped down on that couch that was in the church ladies' bathroom—as it is in all Baptist church ladies' bathrooms—for Jesus-only-knows why. (I later concluded that the reason was obvious—Baptist churches don't have confessionals, and the gossip has to be relayed somewhere.) Meg was moaning and making some awful noises, so I got down and dug in the big cardboard box full of castaway clothes that sat in the corner of the restroom. The GA Castaway Clothes Box was put there by Mrs. Mounts, and she said we were to fill it with old clothes for kids who "cannot afford them." When the box was full, she was going to ship it away to the missionaries' kids in Africa. I thought I might find something to wrap around my head and make Meg laugh. Instead, holy of holies, I found myself a *miracle.*

There, on top of the box, sat a pair of acid-washed Guess blue jeans, just like my cousin Suzanne in junior high had, and just like the pair I had begged Momma for in the middle of Value City the week before. She had said we could not afford them.

I felt the adrenaline—or was it pure, unadulterated Holy Spirit?—course through my body as I lifted the jeans from the box. Like a voice from above, Momma's very words echoed through my head as I read the words Mrs. Mounts had printed on the side of the box—CLOTHES, FOR CHILDREN OF MISSIONARIES OF THE WORD, WHO *CANNOT AFFORD THEM.*

Now, if anyone appreciated the sacrifice of the Baptist foreign missionaries, it was me. But the only missionary's kid I'd ever met at the time was Micah Nichols, the fat-brat son of my daddy's friend from seminary. I had to sit by Micah when my parents had the Nicholses over for supper one night, while

Micah just bragged on and on about how the Southern Baptists paid for his family's huge house down in Africa, and how they had a maid and could spend their money on whatever they wanted. He also said he didn't have to go to school because his momma taught him at home, and the two of them just played all day with his millions of toys that were taken as "castaways" from sucker GAs like me.

When I heard Meg groan again from the stall, right like a voice from the beyond, it reminded me of how Micah had laughed at her for saying the blessing with her eyes open, when she was just a toddler. Right then, I decided I could not let any of the spoiled missionary girls who Micah played with in Africa get their grubby little hands on a pair of brand-new acid-washed Guess jeans. God did not want the bratty little children to be blessed at all, and He was telling me, personally.

If there was any doubt in my heart as to what I should do, it was erased when, through the large crack in the bathroom door that led out into the hallway, I spotted the glowing edge of the church trophy case, full of all the marvelous instruments of ministry. Mrs. Mounts herself had told me that when God called you to be a missionary to the downtrodden, one of the ways you knew it was Him was that He gave you special tools to minister.

Now, fancy clothes may not seem like a very religious tool, but any child who grew up in east-central Kentucky and ever flipped on Channel Three would tell you differently. At age eight, I was convinced that the TV minister lady on Channel Three was the most famous and best lady missionary in the world. And as far as I was concerned, anyone could see it was all because of her beautiful clothes. Every Sunday night,

I tuned in anxiously to see children line up all around her to feel of her furs and play with her fancy beads while she ministered the Word. My mother always said she was nothing but tacky trash and made me turn the channel, but sometimes I would sneak and watch because I was fascinated with the TV lady. I thought her huge, white poofy hair made her head look surrounded in light, like the picture of the angel on the King's Way Baptist nursery wall. I could not imagine a more wonderful life than to look so glamorous, and to be a TV-star servant to the Lord at the same time. I told this to Mrs. Mounts once and she said, "Now, Emy, remember that Lottie Moon was a wonderful missionary as well, and she got by with next to no clothing *or* food." (I wanted to tell Mrs. Mounts that Lottie Moon was *no* kind of missionary anymore because, as we learned in GAs, she was dead of starvation in China. But I bit my tongue.)

I had never been so sure of anything in my life as I was that those jeans could give me the wonder-working power. I could just see my ministry—little poor, pitiful girls in my class at school like Pepsi Moffett would be drawn in by that triangle label on my back pocket.

"Where did you get Guess jeans?" Pepsi would say.

"They were a blessing from the Lord," I would say. "You, child, will be blessed, too, if you will come to church on Sunday."

I lifted those beautiful, almost-white blue jeans from the box. For just a second, I felt a little twinge like I might be doing something wrong, but I decided it must be the Devil trying to talk me down from goodness. After all, I reasoned, if the TV lady was dressing fancy against the will of God, something really awful would have happened to her and her clothes by then.

Then (as if I needed the Lord's additional confirmation) another amazing thing happened. I saw a ball of bright red vinyl sitting square in the middle of the castaway box, just like a burning bush. It was the very thing that Meg threw *her* Value City tantrum over, a red-and-black Michael Jackson jacket with zippers painted on the sleeves. Meg *loved* Michael Jackson, but Momma had looked at that jacket as if it were covered in bird doo and made Meg put it back. Momma had said we could not afford that jacket, either, even though Meg had snatched it from the bargain bin and it was only ninety-nine cents. Now, I was *certain* that just when Meg was sick, walking straight through the Valley of the Shadow of Sunday School Cuisine, God had provided me with this jacket so that I could bestow it on her and lift her soul.

Sure enough, when I ran over to that stall, Meg lit up and jumped straight off the toilet seat. Her face was all red from having her head between her knees, and her pants were still wound up around her ankles, but her little blue eyes were dancing. She put the jacket on and started shaking her little bare butt all around the bathroom.

But then the Devil started tugging at Meg's soul, too.

"Is it really okay if I take this, instead of the mission kids?" she asked me, as if I were the high-authority. I had to give her my high-authority answer, and I told her the truth as well as I knew it—that they didn't even have Michael Jackson in Africa.

"The kids down there would just throw that jacket in the garbage," I told her, and I was proud of the wisdom that God had allowed to come out of my mouth.

The big church bell tolled, telling us it was the end of the church service, and of GAs and RAs and nursery. I was so thrilled to tell Momma about my new gift and how her own daughter was going to be a world-famous missionary that I nearly tore Meg's arm off running through the swinging bathroom door.

Instead I knocked down Mrs. Mounts. She hoisted herself up quickly, making sure that her big wraparound skirt didn't come open.

"Well, my goodness! We need to watch where we're going!" she said.

Meg and I started to mumble that we were sorry, but Mrs. Mounts was already staring down at the castaway clothes in our arms.

"Elizabeth Emerson," she said, "aren't those from the castaway box?" She pointed with her eyes at the denim wad under my arm. She didn't say anything about Meg's jacket, but it was talking loudly enough for itself.

"Mrs. Mounts, it was a *miracle* . . . ," I started to explain, but she shushed me. Daddy was right. Mrs. Mounts thought I was dumb as dirt, just like all God's blessed children and just like her.

She grabbed each of us by the hand and started for the choir room. Mrs. Mounts's hands were covered in slimy lotion, and Meg pulled hers away and wiped it on her dress.

I looked up at Mrs. Mounts's face and was confused. I had seen her get angry in Sunday School before, like the time Davy Marsh spilled paint on her new shoes. She had tried to act like it was an accident and she didn't mind, but her face had gotten as red as her puffy dyed hair. This time, though,

Mrs. Mounts was acting angry, but her face looked calm. Her lips were pursed up tight, the way I did mine when I thought of something inappropriate during church. Mrs. Mounts was not mad; she was excited. She just couldn't wait to tattle on the preacher's kids. And she thought we couldn't tell.

When we got to the choir room, Momma was practicing a solo with Mr. Eddie, the Minister of Music. Mrs. Mounts strode in smiling, just like she was the happiest she'd ever been in her life and Momma was her best friend.

"I just *haaaaaaate* to interrupt this beautiful singing," Mrs. Mounts cooed, stretching out her Kentucky drawl to make it sound Georgia, the way she always did, "but I am afraid . . ."

I blocked out her voice because I couldn't stand it, and I followed Meg over to the chalkboard to draw. I drew all the crosses and manger scenes I could sketch in a minute, so that Momma would look over and see that I was full of the Spirit, and that Mrs. Mounts was full of something else.

But Momma didn't look. She didn't yell, either. She didn't say we were sinful, or anything about Meg and me at all. She just waited until Mrs. Mounts left and said, "I cannot tell you how embarrassed I am."

On the way home, our station wagon was silent as the grave. I told Momma about all the miracles that had guided me to the castaway box, but instead of shushing me like a dummy, she just told me she was *not* a dummy, and that Meg had better quit rolling her eyes. It was not worth the effort to keep trying. Even if I thought there was nothing to be embarrassed about, I knew there was nothing worse than making my mother feel embarrassed in front of church people. As I've said before, we were just as good as royalty on Southern Baptist Sundays. And right then, I felt as if I were Princess Diana and had pulled my dress up over my head during the Easter Pageant while the Queen Mother was up there in the choir loft.

"You are to give those clothes back," Momma said. "You are to write a letter that says you are sorry and give it to Mrs. Mounts. And you will spend tonight's Kentucky game in the guest bedroom, where you will look up the words *thief, ornery,* and *ungrateful* in the dictionary."

And that was the end of that.

That night, Momma did eventually release Meg and me in time to see the last quarter of the ball game. The entire second half, in fact.

But I stayed on in the guest room, on principle. I had to fulfill my Christian duty and transcribe a parable based on my experiences that morning, so that it could one day be used to guide the masses. It was called "The Revenge of the Gucci Ghost," and it was the sad story of an obese church lady (who coincidentally fit Mrs. Mounts's profile to the letter) who taught GAs, and who carried a massive Gucci handbag with her always. Even though, as my mother had told me repeatedly, "A family of four could eat for weeks on what one of those purses cost," the woman in my story carried hers with pride. In fact, the day she bought it happened to be GA "Feed the Five Thousand Day," when GA troops around the country collected donations for the missions hunger effort. This woman thought, perhaps, that she *should* donate to the hunger effort instead of buying the purse, but she reasoned that this could wait. After all, who knew how many ladies in town, starved for the Word, would approach her in admiration of her kid-leather, icon-stamped marvel. Then, with this foothold, her ministry to them could begin. So she bought the purse for five hundred dollars. And meanwhile, on the missions front in China, Lottie Moon was waiting for her plate of rice. But she, a missionary who thought of herself last, was last in the food line behind the hungry masses. And when Lottie finally got to the front, the server told her, "We are so sorry. There is no more food left to give you. We thought there would be, as we were to have a big donation from the King's Way Baptist Church in Kentucky. But for some strange reason, the donation was exactly five hundred dollars short, so we couldn't buy you any rice." And that was the night that Lottie Moon died.

And as for the purse lady, her dreams were tortured for eternity with the rattling ghost of Lottie Moon, who moaned and wailed and asked the purse lady repeatedly why she didn't just take a free purse from the castaway box. *Amen. The End.*

THE THREE FIND-ME-A-BLIND-PERSON MICE

If you are a wandering soul seeking a church home, the first thing any good recruiter will tell you is that Baptist church is free. When the offering plate is passed at you, it's just a suggestion. (In fact, it might be wiser not to drop a big wad of money into it, because then people will wonder just what debt you are trying to settle up with Jesus.) This much is true. What they don't tell you, though, is that there is a toll. And right as you enter the little breezeway that leads into the sanctuary, you'll meet the collectors—the feather-crowned, sharp-toothed, Jungle Gardenia–scented breed known as the Southern Baptist Greeters. Before you can worship in peace, you'll have to survive their cheek-pinching, church-program-slapping, casually-asking-*where-were-you-last-Sunday* gauntlet.

At King's Way Baptist Church, the Greeters were *always* Gladys Cantrell, Betty Burnside, and Henrietta Crane. (And heaven help you if you volunteered to relieve any one of them from her post.) All three of them were real tight with Mrs. Mounts, and they were all about "fixing and doing" for the church. In fact, Daddy called them the Three "Find-Me-a-Blind-Person" Mice. They were best friends with one another, but in a funny way, Daddy said, on account of they were always trying to outdo one another with who could be the most Christian. If one of them brought a bag of groceries to a shut-in (which is the secret church word for someone who is too pitiful to go to the grocery themselves), the other brought a station-wagon-ful. And the third—*dear Lord*, when she got wind of it the poor shut-in would find herself at the center of a kindness maelstrom, after which she'd emerge with twelve turkeys in her fridge (months before Thanksgiving, in the house where she was no longer able to use the stove), her hair and nails done, and a donated evening gown in her tiny closet ("just for a little something fancy!").

The outtakes of the Mice became legendary in short order. Soon rumors of what they were up to, of what gracious hell-fires had burned behind their heavy-blushed, smiling cheeks, started to reach the level of myth. Just like you couldn't always tell where the true kindness stopped and the competition kindness began, where the Mice were concerned it was hard to tell which tales of their exploits were true and which were just parables—legends passed down in whispers at church suppers, until the real story was so buried under mashed potatoes and fried chicken that it wasn't recognizable anymore.

Momma was always quick to shush me whenever I asked her about the truth behind one or the other of the Mice rumors. She always gave me those you-know-better eyes and said that it was one of the "true tragedies of our church" that people would sooner gossip about the good than about the bad. *That might be true*, I always thought, but on the other hand, Mrs. Mounts herself was always talking about how the Bible passages came to be because they were passed down, passed down, and passed down. That meant that *someone* in those olden times was playing telephone tag, *someone* was encouraging the whispering at the church supper, and taking notes. And I bet no one called that person "Gossip." No, she was "Scribe," or "Witness," and the nations rose up and praised her skill. Why, if they didn't, the Bible itself might never have been written.

And that is why I felt comfortable, once or twice, repeating the only Mice story that was powerful enough to stick in my head. I could never remember who first told it to me, or why, and Daddy said he never heard of such a thing happening; that some teenage church nursery worker must have been pulling my leg. But he had laughed. In telling Daddy the story, I'd given him a sermon that he'd never heard. And whether there was truth at the heart of it or not, that fact alone was enough to make my heart rejoice. I decided I'd keep repeating the legend of the day the Mice met Mrs. Monroe.

The whole thing happened when I was in kindergarten, I thought. It all started when the old black man who sat in King's Way's back row, and who was always yelling out "Amen" in the middle of Daddy's sermons, brought his little grandson Kevin to church with him, since Kevin was visiting his grandpa for the month of June. Well, "Glad, Bett, and Hen," as the Mice called themselves, decided the little boy must need saving. First, Glad invited him to the RA group her husband taught, and his grandpa let him go. Glad showed up to sit in on the group that night, and also to give Kevin a Bible and a big handful of pamphlets. Well, before the class was over, in walked Bett with a sack of canned goods for the boy to take home. Right behind her came Hen, with a big bag of castaway clothes that her boy Joe wouldn't wear anymore.

When it became clear that Bett's frankincense and Hen's myrrh had followed Glad's gold, those three got all worked up into a frenzy, because not one of them wanted to come out seeming less gracious than the others. So, since his grandpa hadn't arrived just yet to pick him up, they decided to drag Kevin into the beginning of their Women's Missionary Union meeting, where they would introduce him together as their newest missions project. No sooner had they set up the poor child in front of the sanctuary, surrounded by his cans of Cream-of-Mushroom manna and used swaddling clothes, there came an almighty voice from above:

"Where is the RA group? And *what* in the Devil is going on *here*?"

Only it wasn't from above, but from the back of the sanctuary. And not from the Holy Spirit, but from a tall black woman in a polka-dot dress, the same one Henrietta Crane happened to be wearing.

Her name was Mrs. Carl Monroe, the Women's Missionary Union learned as she climbed a verbal Mount of Olives during her trip down the aisle to her boy. She was Christian. Her father was a fifth-generation minister up north—a fifth-generation *Baptist* minister. Her husband held perhaps the only post higher than the pulpit in Southern Baptist doctrine, that of assistant college basketball coach. And at that college, she herself was a graduate student, not of home economics or even education, but of physics.

When I pictured this story in my head, I thought of Henrietta Crane standing there, hulking over that poor boy who was just a mustard seed to her mountain, frozen in holy terror as Mrs. Monroe came at her like Bobby Knight to an overstuffed referee. And I just bet none of the WMUers rushed to speak up in Hen's defense. I bet they just stared down at the pinholes in their spectator pumps, wishing they would suddenly get large enough for them to crawl into and disappear.

But when she reached the altar, Mrs. Monroe did not raise a chair, like Bobby Knight would have. She did not even raise her voice. Instead she knelt down by her child, whom Mrs. Crane had wrapped in a used and worn winter jacket. She took his hand and turned, as if to preach to the choir that was also the WMU and the Christmas Drive staff and the entire faculty of Sunday School teachers. She said, "Kevin, I am so proud of you for coming here and witnessing to these ladies. And look, you are even in costume to help them with some sort of dramatic presentation. Let me guess . . ."

She put a finger to her chin and glared at Henrietta, who stood frozen to her post behind Kevin, her big hips jutting out round on either side of his head. (Now, I think, would be the opportune time to tell you that Mrs. Crane was the wife of the owner of Crane's Bakery.)

"Hmmm . . . ," Mrs. Monroe continued. "Now, we've got torn and shabby clothes, a mess of half-eaten food, and . . ." She put her hand on Mrs. Crane's shoulder and looked straight into her eyes. "I know! You're acting out the parable of Jonah. Jonah and the *whale*."

And as I have said, I was not there to bear witness, but I will bet that Mrs. Crane just did this little grin with eye bats that I have seen her do before. In fact, it is the same grin that Meg used to do when she pooped in her pants and thought no one could smell it. What did happen (or so I was told) is that Henrietta Crane fainted right as the Monroes left the building, and she had to be rushed to the hospital. She would later say that she just hadn't been feeling well all day. Hadn't been "in her right frame of mind" at all, not at all.

So, as I said, I have no proof that this parable of gossip is true. But I do know that, shortly after it started getting around, the Three Mice seemed to put a damper on their crusading. For about a week.

A few Sundays later they were at it again, posed at the edge of the sanctuary with stacks of programs, just like it was *their* house and *they* were welcoming everyone else in for a dinner party. I bet they wouldn't even let the Lord Jesus inside until He wiped His sandals.

Lesson 2

Misses Ginny and Geneva
Gordon taking the Little
Lambs to the turkey farm

Gentleness

BLUEGRASS LADIES OF FAITH

Little Lambs.

In my first years as a child of the Southern Baptist Church, that's what I was called. My Sunday School classroom door proclaimed it, no matter what church Daddy was preaching in, no matter what corner of Kentucky had asked for his holy expertise. Always sandwiched in the hallway of the church basement, somewhere between the "Fishers of Men" (teenage boys), and the "Adams and Eves" (people your grandparents' age) or the "Marys and Josephs" (young married couples), I was officially part of the only category that didn't even qualify as human in the world of Southern Baptist education. And it was just as well. Every Sunday morning, the teacher who ushered me through that door was usually about twice Methuselah's age, smelled like mothballs, and probably couldn't tell the difference between me and the five hundred or so cats she read scripture to every night. Usually. There were exceptions. And two of these, in particular, I will always credit with setting me on the path to true enlightenment, with opening my eyes to the glory and honor that surrounded a breed of mystics more fantastic to my soul than any Disney princess in tulle, closer and warmer to the touch than the TV lady—true Bluegrass Ladies of Faith.

My first sacred contact with Ginny and Geneva Gordon came on the Sunday after my fourth birthday. It happened to be my father's first Sunday as pastor at white-marble-columned King's Way Baptist. My momma had sobbed in the car all that morning, remembering the little oak-pewed country sanctuary at Grace Baptist where my father had held his first full-time preaching job. It was the church that had filled Momma and Daddy's freezer with casseroles for three solid months after my sister and I were born. It was where, after my mother's purse was stolen from her car during a December choir practice, and her envelope of Christmas shopping money along with it, the whole soprano section ("farmer's wives all of 'em, without a cent to spare," Momma wept) took up a collection and placed the missing money on Momma's chair, without a word. (Years later, I'd understand that there was more to her tears. Preparing for a life in yet another Southern Baptist Church was never an easy task for my mother. The multi-tiered status system of wives and women was a unique and delicate thing in each church. Fitting in would be a nuanced art for anyone; it was especially difficult when you were inserted, out of the blue, to be the new First Lady of them all. I would watch her struggle, with each new church, in front of the mirror for at least an afternoon before one of these first Sunday mornings. *Would this be one of those hats-lady crowds, or no hats? Pumps or Pappagallos? Is our God a stylish God, 'round these parts?*)

I wanted to comfort Momma that morning at King's Way. Daddy had told me that this was an especially hard trip for her, because her own daddy had gone off to be with Jesus. For her, Grace Baptist had gotten to be like that daddy. That was the way it was for a lot of people, and we should not hold it against them, but the rest of us had to be extra strong and brave enough to carry them along. We were headed to King's Way because God had called Daddy there, just like a lottery winner. Not even a million dollars' worth of Grace Baptist casseroles could make us ignore Him.

I appreciated God's almighty will and everything, but for me there was an even greater force of excitement that bubbled in my stomach every Sunday morning of my fourth year, as the grand King's Way steeple pointed its winner's shadow at my family's path. For once, I was going to a real, grown-up Sunday School class. At Grace Baptist, age four was still considered "Nursery Level." Sure, they gave you your own little chair to sit in instead of a floor mat, and you got vanilla wafers for snack instead of a half-gummed box of Cheerios, but there was still that darn SHHHH . . . BABIES INSIDE! sign on the door. And there was the embarrassing ritual, every single Sunday, of your momma slipping the teacher a spare pair of your panties in a plastic bag before class began, "just in case." This came right before a sing-along on a scratchy record player, with rhymes about how big and grown up you were. After that you had to take a nap under one of the cribs.

But there would be no napping whatsoever in the anxious, sunshine-shocked, Sunday-morning-coffee-fueled centrifuge of Ginny and Geneva Gordon, rulers of the King's Way Little Lambs Department. Just to look at the both of them, with their painted fingernails and costume earrings, was enough to keep any child's attention. Momma said the twin Gordon sisters were "ex-debutantes" (which was the Virginia equivalent of princess). And they had once taught in the Kentucky public school system, in the same tiny classroom, though I had a hard time imagining how they survived that way long enough to be put out to pasture in Sunday School Land. Sure, they *looked* alike; from the balcony, you could spot their heads, which were the only two wearing true fur hats, in an instant. But that was about where the sameness ended, and we Lambs noticed it.

For example, while they were both constantly hugging all of us, we all pulled away slightly from Ginny's squeezes. This was because Geneva had a good, soft chest, like any other old lady. Ginny, on the other hand, wore a bra that looked like steel-plated cones under her sweater, and you felt like you were in for a bruising every time she knelt in front of you. Ginny also had big, fluffy hair wrapped into a thick French twist that reminded me of melted chocolate, while Geneva's hair was thin-to-invisible in places. She carried her head as if she had a bouffant-to-the-floor, though; as if her hair was the way luxurious hair was *supposed* to look, didn't we all know that?

They were sort of opposite in the way they taught us, too ("Polar opposites," I'd heard one of the Sunday School board members tell Daddy, when Daddy told him I was entering Little Lambs, "sort of the Cain and Abel of the Sunday School world, God love 'em"). Ginny poured out sweetness like it was holy water. She seemed convinced that all children needed to be spoken to in song, with each vowel drawn out for ten or fifteen minutes. Her song-message would get longer and longer if the news she was delivering to us was dark (as if she meant to bore us so numb we wouldn't feel the truth), and it got gradually higher in pitch as she reached the bad parts. Her highest-ever falsetto came one Sunday morning when Miss Phoebe, the church cafeteria lady who usually came to stock our cups with orange drink, failed to show up during Sunday

School hour. When Angela Rudolf asked Miss Ginny where she was, Ginny almost screeched, "Well, dear. You see, Jeeesus likes to take in new angels, from tiiiime to time, picked especially from his veeeeeeeeery best servants—"

"Oh cool it, Ginny," Geneva interrupted, smiting her sister on the forehead with a rolled-up song sheet. "Honey," she went on, moving her glasses to the end of her nose, "Phoebe keeled over in the Fellowship Hall soup tureen yesterday. Now she's dead, and yes, she is in heaven."

But the Gordon sisters came into their fullest and most righteous glory when they were in harmony, seated at the head of our tiny-chaired circle for the morning's lesson. Here were women who took soul saving seriously, and I knew it. My nursery teachers before them mostly just read us the watered-down gospel from the Sunday School teacher's manual, with stories about how one mouse stole the other mouse's cheese and made the first mouse feel sad. (I suppose the cheese was supposed to be "salvation"? Some of those early parables were insulated with coats of sugar so thick that it was hard to imagine how anyone, much less most four-year-olds, could figure out what they were really getting at.)

But not the Gordons; no, they wouldn't touch that manual. Many a time, I skipped the midlesson snack break because I just couldn't tear myself away from their private, powerful pulpit. Ginny spoke of how Jesus had held her and lifted up her family through bad crops, and through fevers that used to pluck children our age right from their beds and into heaven. Geneva found us a diagram showing the massive stomach capacity of the great blue whale, and told us it was as tough-skinned as a basketball, and could easily stretch to hold a man

Jonah's size inside it. Both the Gordons spoke to us as if we were just as entitled to a good sermon as our parents were.

And then there came the moment when heaven shone down and truly illuminated the sisters for the faithful angels that they were—the infamous Gordon Sunday School Field Trip of Thanksgiving 1984.

Miss Ginny and Miss Geneva had arranged, the Sunday before the holiday, to take all the Little Lambs on a post-church trip to see a real working turkey farm. The whole thing was very religious, of course. We spent that entire Sunday morning learning to be thankful to God for creating the beasts of the field and the birds of the air, and we marveled over the stuffed-and-mounted turkey hunt trophy Miss Ginny's husband brought in to show us, before praying for its soul.

After church, our mothers changed us out of our dress clothes into play clothes in the Fellowship Hall, and Misses Ginny and Geneva went into the ladies' room to change their own clothes. As Momma was pulling down my sweater cuffs, which had gotten all scrunched up underneath my coat sleeves, I heard Angela Rudolf gasp.

There, at the ladies' room door, my teachers had emerged—in *pants*. Both wore wide, elastic-waisted polyester pants, and not a one of us had ever seen them that way. I suppose you really had to be a Southern Baptist child, raised immune to the eternally ruffled, magnolia-scented monoliths that were the elder church ladies, to appreciate how fascinated we were at the sight. It was like seeing a poodle come walking through the grocery store, pushing a cart on its hind legs—within possibility, but just barely.

When we got to the turkey farm, Misses G and G led us

single file to a large, closed barn, the first stop on the big tour. I had positioned myself at the front of the line, of course, for I assumed that if my teachers were for some reason unable to continue the class, it would fall upon me to take the reins.

I stood behind Miss Geneva as she lifted the large beam that held the door closed. Behind me, excited giggles rippled through the line. *You will get to see where it all begins*, Miss Geneva had told us on the bus ride over. She had asked us to close our eyes and painted marvelous, poetic pictures of God striking thunderbolts of life into a single, fragile eggshell.

The giggles got louder as she opened the door, just a crack. Suddenly Miss Geneva gasped. She gave Miss Ginny an urgent look.

I bent under Miss Geneva's arm to get a look through the crack. Maybe, I thought, there were so many thunderbolts of life going off inside that it just wasn't safe for kids to enter yet.

But my nose told me, even before my eyes did, that this was not the case. Through the door crack, I made out the forms of hundreds of dead, headless turkeys, lying in rows.

Now, why it never occurred to my teachers that the nature of a turkey "farm" might make it unsuitable for children, I still don't know. Call it the trait of blessed obliviousness that made certain women ideally suited to teach Southern Baptist Lambs. But in the moment when I stared, openmouthed, up at Miss Ginny, she knew it was too late. One child had seen the truth through the crack in the door. And in the pre-kindergarten-aged group, that was the same as if all the children had seen through it.

And that's when Miss Ginny made the most graceful, divinely inspired gesture I've ever seen. She bent low to all the children, put a finger to her mouth, and whispered:

"The turkeys are having nap time! Let us tiptoe quietly through the barn. Let us sing them all a lullaby!"

And so it came to pass that on a crisp Sunday afternoon, I and my twenty-three classmates tiptoed, heads bowed, singing "Onward Christian Soldiers," through the largest collection of turkey carcasses in Kentucky. Such was the saving grace of my leaders. Now *that* was an education in faith; *those* were Sunday School teachers. Two sacred members of the seldom-seen order of Bluegrass Ladies of Faith.

As I saw them both silhouetted in the sunny tunnel of light that marked the exit of the barn, I knew I was seeing two of the rarest women I'd ever encounter in my Christian life, even if I lived to be as old as they were. This was to be expected, Daddy would later say, because very few people were actually called by the Heavenly Father to teach Sunday School. Most just got guilted into it (and thank heaven for sin, or there would be no Sunday School educators at all).

But it seemed to me, that day, that it was more. What I'd seen as the Gordons walked ahead of me—forgive me, Lord, but I was sure about it—wasn't anybody being called by anything, pulled by anything, ordered by anyone or any man. Misses Ginny and Geneva seemed driven by a light that came from deep inside them; it pushed their heads up and their eyes forward. It never doubted that an entire warehouse of dead turkeys could be resurrected with a smile, a march in time, and a hum on the pitch pipe. And though it came out of the oldest, littlest women I knew, it was the most powerful thing I'd ever felt. I'd never tell Daddy about it, because it seemed like a blasphemous thought. I just thought about it quietly in bed that night, with the souvenir turkey feather that I'd always regard as a holy relic, hidden beneath my pillow.

Maybe this, I thought, as I drifted to sleep, peaceful and safe in the world of the Gordons, maybe this was why the sisters had stayed in the Little Lambs Department for thirty years. Maybe they knew that this gentle time in our lives was a thing to be savored, because for Bluegrass Baptist women of faith, it could be snatched without any notice. You could be walking along at any time and hit a barn door, strangely locked. But you'd have to go on, forward. You'd need to put your chin up to the world and hold your nose. And your soul would need to grow calluses faster than you'd ever expected.

THE MEEK SHALL INHERIT THE F WORD

There were many people, Daddy said, who worshipped much higher on the meekness spectrum than the Gordon sisters; those who thought child-like innocence should be not only nurtured but also preserved into adulthood. There were some, he said, who had all but advocated for a Middle-Aged Lambs Sunday School class.

The head advocate at King's Way was Mrs. Lynndale Pence, as everyone knew. It was easy to pick her out in the hallway, I thought, because she pretty much dressed like a Little Lamb, even though she was a grown-up. All her skirts had really thick petticoats, and I always thought her frilly jumpers looked a lot like Meg's pinafores. You could have easily mistaken Mrs. Pence for an overgrown preschooler if it weren't for the fact that she was pregnant most of the time.

One Sunday afternoon, I'd been playing under the tall-back love seat in Daddy's church study, waiting for him to finish up his after-church business, when I overheard Mrs. Pence—near tears—come in moaning about language that was "decidedly too adult" being used in the nursery. When Daddy asked her what she meant by "too adult," she wouldn't say. And when he asked her what words, in particular, she still wouldn't say. But she finally did whisper, after steadying her shaking self against an armchair, that the too-adult term she was speaking of was "the F word."

I felt my body recoil farther back under the couch. It was true that I didn't know what "the F word" was, specifically. But I did know it existed, out there in the dangerous universe of things that made you a sinner just by hearing or seeing them, even if it was by accident (like the MTV channel my babysitter sometimes flipped past, too slowly).

"The F word?" Daddy said, dropping his pencil in midsentence. "*The* F word. You're sure about this?"

Mrs. Pence nodded. She looked like she might collapse, so great had been the burden of waiting to tattle on whoever had said the swear.

"One of the little ladies who keeps the nursery said the F word. That's what you're telling me."

"Yes, Reverend. It pains me to tell it, but many, many times it was said. By someone. I hate to name any names . . ."

"Well, then let's not for right now—"

". . . but it was said by Suzette Volpenheim."

"Suzette Volpenheim?" Daddy said. I wondered if his eyebrows might just raise far enough to hit the line of his hair. Why he hadn't asked me to leave the room yet, I wasn't sure, but maybe he thought that if a matter had not yet been officially declared "too adult," then I, mature for my age as I was, had a perfect right to listen in.

"Well, hold on then, let me take down the details," Daddy said, grabbing a special pink notepad from the shelf next to his desk. It was the secret pad he used for church complaints. I always got excited when I saw him take it out; it was like he got to play police.

"Now, you say Suzette Volpenheim—and that's the Suzette Volpenheim who's nine months pregnant and runs the Christian day care down on Old Mill Road—she has been spouting off the F word in front of the kids?"

Mrs. Pence nodded, slow and deep as if with a hymn. Daddy stopped writing for a second. He put down his pen. His eyes narrowed, the way they always did when he asked me to explain my actions when I was in trouble, and he knew that something in my story didn't seem quite right.

"Mrs. Pence, forgive me. But just so I can be sure we've got the details right for when I act on this. Would you mind spelling the F word for me? I mean, it's not as if a minister is well versed in this sort of vocabulary."

She leaned forward, about as far over Daddy's desk as she could go without falling over. I could see a little bit up under her dress from where I was, and I wondered why anyone would need to wear three slips at the same time.

"Well, it's . . . it's . . . ," she whispered, but loud enough to hear. When church ladies came in to tell Daddy gossip, they always had a special way of whispering all dignified-like, but in such a way that you could still hear it three blocks away.

". . . it's . . . F . . . A . . . R . . . T."

Daddy told me, later on, that it was bad manners of him to laugh out loud at Lynndale Pence and then try to cover it up by coughing. He said that it was just funny to him how the definition of *adult* seemed to change when you walked through the door of the church. It was part of the whole "dumb as dirt" thing. People wanted to take the Bible's order that we be "little lambs" before God literally, so everyone had to act like we were all as pure and innocent as four-year-olds.

Of course, despite all this, he said that I still had to say "fluff" instead of "fart." And that I couldn't let on that I knew that Suzette Volpenheim was about to be fired from nursery duty. Daddy said he really had no choice, unfortunately. The preschool Little Lambs probably carried the least amount of clout of any member of the congregation. But the Big ones would always be a different story.

Lesson 3

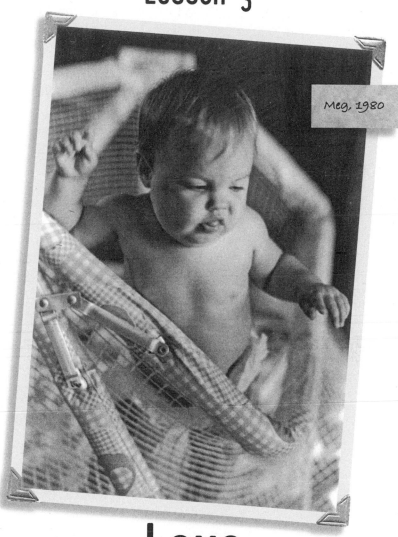

Meg, 1980

Love

BRANCHES

All Sunday School teachers love the lesson about Jesus being some sort of gardener; about how He is the vine and we are the branches, and the branches spout out from the vine like one big family tree. (Though you must never raise your hand and ask if that means Jesus had his own wife and kids, because this is a blasphemy. He just turned into a big old tree for fun and that's it, and if you are stupid enough to refuse to leave it at that, your teacher will tell your parents that you need to watch less television.) I always thought they liked the tree lesson because even the dumbest of little kids could draw a decent tree, and that meant even the laziest of teachers could sit back during craft time and let her nails dry.

On those fall Sunday mornings, the teacher always brought in a pile of dead leaves, a handful of stale-brown crayons, and some ancient glue that had hardened to a permafrost, and asked us to create our own tree, "a vision of eternal growth in Christ." Instead I sat down in the corner, prayed a silent prayer for guidance, and opened my Bible notebook. There I constructed in my own words the most glorious vision of "God's Favorite Branches." I wrote about one branch in particular that grew far and slender, and was crowned with flowers and wrapped with rope swings that could almost reach as far as heaven. The branch had the most tender of green hearts. Fruit fell from its boughs for the hungry, and shade fell down like cool rain upon the weary. If two teenagers met under the branch to try to kiss (as hell-bound teenagers sometimes did), the branch would come down and scratch up the girl's face so that the boy wouldn't want to kiss her anymore, and then both would be saved.

Yes, it was a marvelous branch, indeed. But it was not alone on the vine. One day, while God was not paying attention to pruning, a smaller branch—something like a little tree wart—poked its way out underneath the grand branch. And the Mother and Father branches up above said, "What a beautiful branch! It is at least as strong and as good as the grand branch above it." Of course, anyone could see that they were mistaken, because the new branch was lower and newer than the grand branch, and therefore could not get as much heavenly light, and could not be as strong. It was a scientific fact (and plants are always the science of God, even if animals like monkeys are not).

When God chanced upon the little wart-branch one day, He smiled on it because He had to, even though it was so, so pitiful. He shook His head and sighed, and He patted the leaves. And God hath named that branch "the Sibling Branch."

My little sister Meg poked her fat little head into the world right as I was old enough to appreciate being the only child of the best pastor in town. My presence, I thought, was ordained by the Lord to give the other kids something to aspire to. Having *two* daughters of the most-high just confused things. But there she came a-knocking on my mother's tummy, right before my father was to take the stage one Sunday morning. Because Meg insisted on early labor, everyone at Grace Baptist was kept from hearing the merciful Word of the Lord that week. I decided it was most definitely a harbinger of things to come.

Not that Margaret Gates Hancock ever *tried* to take the spotlight, or the pulpit. No, what bothered me something awful was the fact that she didn't seem interested at all in the important role she was destined, by birth, to play in the spiritual welfare of our community. She was supposedly entirely normal and healthy, but I could see that, in fact, Meg's senses seemed to be broken. She didn't react to the pungent singe of hellfire in her nostrils as it seethed from the mouths of the elders all around us. Nor did pride seem to seep in through her pores, the way it did mine, when they touched the leather of a pew Bible with our grandfather's name in front; or the pages of the Choir Cookbook, with Momma's chicken casserole at top billing; or the scratchy-white newness of an Easter pinafore. She avoided Barbies like the Antichrist, and scurried away from my tea-party invitations so quickly you'd have thought I was inviting her to a leper colony.

No, Meg's senses responded to a far less holy trinity: the dirt; the driveway; and Waylon Jennings (she could barely fall asleep without listening to him). And even then, you couldn't be sure she was actually responding, because she wouldn't say so. The thing that made me feel most separated from my sister was the fact that she didn't talk. And I mean, *at all*. A year passed after her birth, and she hadn't so much as uttered a babble. Then, almost two years. As the time passed between us in silence, Meg became more and more like an alien to me, the child who, in Daddy's words, "came out of the womb preaching."

I couldn't understand it. Meg shouldn't have been that different from me, I knew, because she was part of our family tree. We had the same roots and sap; blooming and blood and seasons. As the months passed from the time when I first met her, I kept watch over her, waiting for the moment when God would make our branches touch and connect and bond; would at least show me where and how they were going to intertwine, or when she was going to talk to me, or play dolls with me. But Meggie grew straight out toward the sun and never bent, not even toward the shelter.

When nearly a year and a half of Meg's life had passed without a word, Momma took her to Dr. Baker to be checked out. But he said she was just fine, and in fact "very social" for her age. She just had her own different ways of communicating, and if we'd only watch closely, we'd know what she was "saying" after all. Her eyes, he said, were especially expressive. In any event, Meg would talk in her own time, and we should all let nature take its course.

But to at least one good church lady, our babysitter Miss Bessie, Meg's "talking eyes" may not necessarily have been the Lord's natural doing. One day, when Bessie had been keeping Meg by herself because I had Cherub Choir practice at church, she came out to Momma's car, holding out my sister away from her body the way you might carry a bread loaf that had gone moldy out to the trash. Meg did not seem to appreciate this; the folds of fat around her neck were jammed up around her earlobes, and she was grunting to beat the band. Momma got out of the car and ran to meet them halfway up the lawn.

"The baby!" Bessie spouted, trying to turn Meg so that her own arms stayed close enough together to keep her housecoat closed. "Missus Hancock, the baby's lookin' like . . . like an adult, today. I mean it, her eyes has got the looks of an adult, look! Look!"

My momma took baby Meg and held her at some distance from her own body, so frightened did Miss Bessie seem of my little sister. But then I could see from the car window exactly what Bessie was shouting about. Meg's shoulders heaved and she let out a long sigh, but then her chin dropped and her head seemed to wiggle back and forth. And then—my heart turned a green so bright I could feel it when I saw it happen—Meg's gray-blue eyes did a perfect roll, then her forehead raised as if to say, *Are we finished here?* I had been trying to master that move since I'd seen my mother do it, on the phone with the parent of one of her pupils. I'd asked Momma how she did it, but she'd said she didn't know what I was talking about.

It was an incredible sight, but odd; like seeing Miss Bessie wearing real shoes, not house slippers. At the same time, I felt that it was something I should have known Meg Hancock would do. If I had the slightest idea who Meg Hancock was. As time had gone by and we'd spent more hours together—as Aunt Kit had made us countless paint-penned trash cans and cross-stitched wall hangings that proclaimed BEST SISTERS, BEST FRIENDS—I didn't have the heart to tell anyone that I didn't know my little sister. It seemed easier to "know" Jesus Christ. You just had to say you knew Him and get baptized and you were as good as brothers.

Brothers. Maybe it's always different with sisters, I thought. *Maybe even God doesn't understand how sisters are supposed to work.*

But even if He didn't understand when He made them, He would find a way to make them work. I didn't come to know this truth until I was almost five years old and Meg was almost three. She didn't come to preach it to me, because she still wasn't speaking. But Dr. Baker was right—she *was* talking. Lord, I didn't see it until heaven's beams shone through the painted glass of Jerry's restaurant on I-75 one afternoon. They lit up my sister's famous eyes, and I saw inside them for the first time.

That morning, Momma had gone off to teach school, leaving Meg and me at home with Daddy. This normally would have been fine, but the timetable of a higher power interfered right before Daddy was supposed to feed us our lunch and give us naps.

Meg had started her usual noon whine-groan—which was a sure sign that she needed her crib like the Devil needs an air conditioner—when the phone rang. Daddy was burning grilled cheese, but still answered the phone in so highfalutin a manner that I was sure the caller assumed he'd been ironing altar cloths all day.

The callers were, I'd learn in a few minutes when the frenzy began, Thad Richards and Jed Turner. Now, Jed Turner I did not know, though Daddy had shown me his picture before in the *Western Recorder*, which is the big Baptist newspaper. Thad was in there a lot, too, but I couldn't think of him as quite so famous, since he'd been in our house several times and once tried to show me a magic trick that didn't work. I liked Thad a lot, but you cannot be a minister and mess up things like magic tricks in front of children. You also cannot let your undershirt show through your top on Sunday mornings. People will think you are flawed.

The two men, Daddy said, worked for the Convention,

which was something like the president but for the church, and consisted of a whole bunch of men rather than just one. (The Catholics had just one, I knew, but I thought this was a silly idea, because what if he turned out to be lying to everyone? The Baptists have many men instead. This is much safer.) Momma also said that the Convention had been trying for a long time to "get Daddy in." This sounded like a good thing to me, because who wouldn't want to be sought after by the bosses of all the churches? But Momma usually didn't smile when she talked about it. She seemed like she wanted to, like she knew she should, but she didn't. She made it sound like getting picked by the Convention was like getting socks for Christmas.

Good or bad, though, Daddy couldn't ignore any call that came from above. Thad and Jed needed to meet him for lunch, he said, and it was urgent. They said that Meg and I could come along, since it was too late for Daddy to find someone to keep us, and Momma was busy in her classroom.

He dumped the blackened grilled cheese in the garbage can, against Meg's shrieks, and hoisted her, kicking, from the high chair. He told me I should get dressed, and fast. It was one of the hottest days of the summer, so Meg was just wearing her diaper and T-shirt. I had on my favorite bathing suit and a tutu.

Though I considered myself quite capable of standing in for Momma at an important pastoral dinner, I was almost hysterical as I tried to decide what to wear. I had never even dressed myself for a Sunday morning before, much less a special occasion, and this was the most special I could have imagined.

Finally, I squashed myself into the closet and slid sideways toward the back, where the plastic bag hung. Inside was my

Christmas dress, bought just for a Cherub Choir recital. It was pink-and-gray taffeta and velvet, and it had a little jingle bell sewn into the hem. It was perfect. The gray shoes I'd worn with it were too tight, so I just left my ballet slippers on.

When I went into Meg's room to get help tying my sash, Daddy was trying to wrestle my sister, who was now purply red and squalling, into a jumper dress on the changing table. She looked like a live sausage. I knew he thought about saying something about the fact that I was wearing my Christmas dress, but after Meg started pummeling him with her feet, he tied my sash without saying a word and told me to wait in the living room.

I sat on the couch and tried to be still. The little bell on my skirt was jingling like crazy in time with my jitters. To tell the truth, the dress was starting to feel scratchy and hot, but I had once heard Momma comment that a dress of Princess Diana's looked scratchy and hot. This reassured me that the dress was the right choice. Princess Diana was almost as glamorous as the TV lady.

After a few more bumps and squalls from down the hall, Daddy and Meg finally emerged. Daddy looked like he'd come in from a windstorm, but was handsome as ever in a tan sport coat, with what looked like a fresh round bite mark on the sleeve. Meg looked calm as could be, almost smiling. The jumper dress was nowhere in sight. Daddy had only succeeded in getting her into an old pair of purple corduroy play pants, with snaps going up the inseam in a way that I would have found most embarrassing had I been her age. On top, her I'M A LITTLE KENTUCKY WILDCAT T-shirt was stretched pretty far, but didn't quite cover her belly.

And as for her head, Meg didn't really have enough hair

for a style yet, but Momma always found a way to make it lie flat when we went out in public. Daddy had only managed to comb half of it over to one side, securing it with a mismatched barrette.

"My hair, Daddy?" I pleaded. He'd already gotten the car keys out of his pocket, so I knew my chances for achieving maximum beauty were slim, but I had to try. After all, hairstyling wasn't an unusual task for Daddy. Since Momma left early for school in the mornings, Daddy always fixed my hair on the days when I went to play school. I always tried to tell him he was just as good as Mommy, even though he wasn't. But he was getting better. So far, he had learned the ponytail and the bun, and was beginning to master braiding, sort of. He had started telling me to never tell the deacons that he knew how to French-braid hair, or else he'd be run out of the Baptist pulpit. I was never sure whether he was joking when he said that or not.

"Well," he said, looking at his watch. "We've got a little time, and your mother would kill me if I didn't at least try. Come on."

He put Meg down like a sack of yams into her playpen, and we went into Dad's Beauty Parlor.

"What will it be today, Miss Em?" he said. I put my finger to my chin as if I was thinking hard, but I knew exactly what was needed for this special day.

"Hmmmm . . ."

I reached into the cup on the sink and pulled out my Princess Leia toothbrush.

"This."

"Oh, honey, that's ambitious . . . ," Daddy said.

I tried to live up to my grown-up dress and not pout, but I couldn't help it. I was going to attend a Convention lunch at Jerry's on I-75, and come hell or broken high chairs, I was going to look dignified. My breath shortened, and I watched my chest heave in the mirror as Daddy's face tightened. We could hear Meg grunting in the other room.

Now, Reverend, do you want one heathen-looking child or do you want two?

Daddy reached into the drawer, into territory he had never sought before—Momma's bobby pin box.

I shut my eyes tight as he worked, fast and furious. I wanted to look, but I couldn't. I wanted to be surprised at the end, like in the movies when the plain girl opens her eyes to find herself transformed into a princess.

Finally Daddy said, "Ta-da! Pretty good, if you ask me."

I opened one eye at a time, slowly. But not slowly enough.

I could tell from the general shape that Daddy had tried, really tried. And at age four, my physical and spiritual health depended upon Daddy not failing, above all else. But my head looked like two birds' nests had exploded out of either side.

I realized—too late—that the mirror hadn't allowed me a moment to adjust my expression before Daddy saw it. He started pressing on the birds' nests, as if to shrink them, but it didn't work.

"You see, honey," he said, wielding a comb that was useless. He had dropped into his sermon voice. "I couldn't do the hairdo like the picture because, well . . ."

He seemed to be conjuring with the comb now. He moved it in the air like a wand. And then he stopped.

"I couldn't do it just like the picture, because Princess Leia is vain. We can't be vain in front of the Convention spokespeople, can we?"

I shook my head. No, I surely did not want to be. I thought

of Meg, sweating through her old clothes in the other room. By Daddy's logic and the way she looked, it was quite possible they might think she was the less vain, holier sister.

"This," Daddy went on, "this is just more suitable for a good girl. Princess Leia has those big rolls, but what you've got is just a little more understated, a little more Kentucky Baptist Convention. Not rolls but . . . but biscuits! You've got custom head-biscuits, and I think they're dandy."

And if my daddy's speech had never turned bread into gold before, Lord if it didn't do so in that bathroom. Suddenly I felt like the most glamorously modest, most flawedly perfect preacher's daughter ever to sit in a plastic booth.

I was so confident, in fact, that when Daddy introduced us to Thad and Jed in the parking lot, I primly reminded them, "My name is Elizabeth Emerson Hancock. And I am wearing biscuits."

"Oh!" Jed said. "Why that's . . . that's lovely. Just lovely."

He said lovely like *luuv-leh*. I practiced saying it the same way under my breath, all the way to our table.

Throughout lunch, I reminded myself over and over that I had to look nonvain in front of these men. When the waitress brought crayons, I stuck only to the ugliest colors as I filled in the Fun Book. I decided I would wait till later to ask Daddy why *I* had to wear flattened biscuits while Thad Richards had enough gold Deacon, Brotherhood, Gideon, and Mission pins on his lapel to make his jacket hang lopsided.

For now, though, I thought Daddy's important lunch was going perfectly. Even Meg, who usually managed to wriggle nearly out of her seat after a few minutes in front of any sort of important people, was quietly making a paste out of her crackers.

I filled in my Fun Book (which wasn't that much fun, and had a boy and girl playing with animals inside the zoo cages, which you aren't allowed to do), and wished that I could talk to her. I wished that she'd talk back, and that we could be like Momma and Kit, or my cousins Suzanne and Dottie Jane, or any of the other sisters I knew, who whispered back and forth in code over macaroni and cheese. If I was going to not like her or get into fights with her, that would have been okay, too. At least I would know enough to *know* I didn't like her. God had given me a gift in a new sister, everyone always said. But He wouldn't let me open it.

What I wouldn't understand until later was that Meg wasn't made to let anyone else open her. She didn't want anyone to speak for her, and she didn't want anyone to speak with her until she was ready. But she would make her feelings known, nonetheless.

There was silence at the table while the waitress took the menus away. She'd left Meg and me with a pair of plastic puppets, but I hadn't touched mine, because I knew Meg wouldn't watch if I tried to entertain her.

Thad looked at Jed, and the two of them slid around in their seats. Finally, after looking around the restaurant as if he was checking for spies, Jed cleared his throat and spoke low at Daddy. It seemed like something important was happening. Even Meg had stopped coloring. She was sucking on a crayon, staring at Jed.

"Reverend Hancock," he said, "the reason we're here today is, well, several things . . . you seem to have your finger on the pulse of the average congregation and . . . well . . ."

He went on for a minute or two, talking about church business that I didn't understand. I went back to coloring, but

Meg didn't. She was still staring. She had managed to wriggle one leg around the outside bar of her high chair, so that her dirty shoe hung directly over my pretty church dress. I decided to ignore this, so long as she did't touch it.

Jed went on, and my ears caught the tail end of what he was saying.

". . . and now, down at Southside, well," he said. Then he stopped, like he couldn't go on. Thad picked it up.

"They're talking about putting a *woman* in the pulpit."

The whole table went silent. I couldn't figure out why, at first. I'd never seen a lady preacher, other than on TV, but I'd always thought that was probably my calling. It didn't seem like a strange idea.

Maybe I'd heard Thad wrong, I thought. Maybe he'd said *werewolf* in the pulpit, not *woman*. Everyone was acting like he'd said *werewolf.*

Meg was still staring, but harder. I hoped she wouldn't start squalling now. She was too little to learn about werewolves. Her eyes looked calm, but her face was getting redder.

I decided to distract everyone. I would tell them about my plan to be the next TV lady. They would be awed and excited, and everyone would forget all about that werewolf and barely notice if Meg decided to turn into a ragamuffin in the nicest restaurant along the highway.

But then it happened. Meg spoke to Thad Richards. Not out loud, though.

The statement came out and fell against the ruffle of my dress. Daddy and the men were huddled deep in conversation, so Meg and I were the only ones who saw it happen.

A golf-ball-size turd had been deposited upon the plastic

pew of the booth. I knew right away that Meg had probably been aiming at a different target, but her pant leg wasn't long enough.

I looked at the offering and I looked up at my sister. The red was gone from her face, and she wore another adult look that said, *Well, there you have it. And what are you going to do about it now?*

A crayon hung out of the corner of her mouth like a cigar, and her eyes flickered toward the Convention spokesmen.

I took a sip of my milk and tried to remain dignified. Daddy was talking up a storm about something that was making his own face turn red. He couldn't be embarrassed, and I knew it; not now, not in front of the Convention.

I leaned over and tugged on his sport coat.

"Now, Miss Em, just a minute. The grown-ups are talking," he said. If only he knew. It wasn't just the grown-ups who were talking.

I tugged again. This time he tapped my knee under the table, in a way that usually meant *you had better watch it.* I didn't want to sass or get a spanking, but this was dire. I pulled harder, and this time I didn't stop when he shushed me.

Finally, Daddy leaned over and said, "For heaven's sake, what is it?"

I didn't want to utter a bathroom word. I whispered in his ear, "Look what Meg has done."

And my father's face, which a moment ago had been full of all the fury of the pulpit, was now white as eternal death. Thad and Jed didn't notice; they'd gone back to mumbling to each other as if Daddy had never been there.

Daddy looked at Meg, who chose not to apologize to him

with her eyes, even though he knew she was capable. Then his eyes searched the table for some way out. Suddenly he looked hopeful. He turned back and, as he answered a question Thad had asked, slipped on my plastic puppet. Then, still talking, firing scripture as if it were perfectly natural to handle poop at the same time, Daddy picked up Meg's offering, turned the puppet inside out, and slipped the whole thing into his suit pocket.

Jed sipped his iced tea and winked at Meg. He commented again on what a cute little lady she was.

On the way home, Daddy stopped at a Dumpster to empty his pocket. Then he got back in the car, stared at Meg in the rearview, and laughed until tears rolled down his cheeks. He made us promise that we would never tell Momma about what happened, and we didn't. It was our secret.

But the bigger secret was what I had felt coming from my sister's eyes that day as she talked to me for the first time from her chair on high—that she wouldn't be kept silent from any pulpit, anytime, anywhere. And unless I wanted to wear a stain on all my church dresses from then on, she'd make sure I didn't settle for silence, either.

JOSEPH AND THE MCALPIN'S BARGAIN-BASEMENT BLAZER

My Memaw once told me that love and charity went hand in hand, and this was one of the most important things you had to understand about being a good church member. Yes, Jesus was dirt poor. And yes, people who are rich are no better than people who are dirt poor. But this does not take away from the fact that if you really want to show that you love someone, you have to give them things. You take up collections, you sell pies and homemade rolls, and you give, give, give, give until you have not an ounce of love left in your heart for their dirt-poor self. Then you will know what it really feels like to be a Christian.

I myself was forced to learn the joyful-painful importance of Christian giving when I was just a toddler and tried to take in a stray cat from our front yard. Momma and Daddy let me keep her long enough to name her Petunia, but not much longer. Because across town, at some farm that God forgot, a pitiful little poor girl had been hoping and praying for a cat just like Petunia, and wouldn't I be a great little missionary if I gave my first pet to her? The experience kind of ruined me for being a cheerful giver, though I never told anyone. I kept up the motions like everyone else. But not nearly to the same extent.

By our second summer at King's Way, Mrs. Joetta Mounts was in the grip of one of the all-time great love-giving frenzies—gushing like a Miss America contestant, weeping about how the crown had to go to her because the good Lord Jesus wouldn't trust anyone else to feed the five thousand using only crushed roses and a rhinestone headdress. Mrs. Mounts had baked for five hundred and won a spot on the hallway bulletin board. She'd held a cake auction for two hundred and earned a picture in a Baptist newsletter. Finally, on the hottest August Sunday I can ever remember, she decided to shower those of us in the Young Shepherds Sunday School class with her charity.

For weeks, our whole class had been in an uproar over the upcoming church picnic, where everyone would have a part in putting on a play about Bible people. Normally, this would involve just throwing on some old burlap sacks and sweating out in the church parking lot while everyone in the audience ached for Joe Crane to finally get through the word *Zechariah* so they could eat their green bean casserole. This year, however, an abundance of little boys wanted to play Joseph in a coat-of-many-colors reenactment. Now, Mrs. Mounts did not want to pick one, since that would suggest favoritism (of course, she had favoritism, she just did not want to suggest it), and she didn't want to pick a name out of a hat, because that was tantamount to gambling. So she decided to have each interested little boy go home and work on a Joseph costume, and then a special nonbiased judge would pick the best one to be Joseph. It seemed fair, especially since that "just ask and it shall be given to you" rule has never especially applied to the honor of being church superstar.

Of course, after a week's worth of He-Man cartoons, most of the boys decided it wasn't so cool after all to make believe you were an old dead carpenter. The only two contestants left were Teddy Banks and Matt Keith. (Matt's daddy, Mr. Keith, was a clear favorite of Mrs. Mounts. He was the youngest of the deacons, and had donated umpteen dozen jerseys to the church softball team, with his insurance firm's logo on the back. Such a great sacrifice, all in the name of the sacred arena of church athletics, was met with greater reverence than any blood drive or build-a-thon I ever witnessed.)

Well, on the Sunday of the judging, Matt strode in wearing a multicolored satin thing trimmed with glittery bric-a-brac. His momma took in sewing, and it was clear to everybody he hadn't made this all by himself according to the rules. It was something to see, though, the headpiece especially. It was made out of a dyed silk that Mr. Keith had brought back from a church trip to India. Matt's momma had sewn little plastic coins all around a sweatband to make the headband. Even Matt's sandals had little costume jewels glued all over them. Daddy peeked through the Sunday School door that morning and later asked Momma whose idea it was to dress up little church boys like the Whore of Babylon.

The only other competition was Teddy Banks, standing there nearly burned to a crisp in the glare given off by Matt's glorious costume, wearing an old bathrobe of his daddy's and a towel on his head.

Mrs. Mounts spent all morning doting over Matt and how "hard he had worked." Then, all of a sudden, she clasped her hands and said, "Well, I am so glad I am not the judge because I just don't know who on earth I would choose!"

Right, and she just didn't know whether Santa would come this year if we misbehaved.

A heavy knock at the door broke the pretend air of suspense. Mrs. Mounts shrieked that the very special judge had arrived, and ran for the door as if Ed McMahon would be standing on the other side. He was not.

There in the doorway, shaking for some reason, was Mr. Nick, the church janitor. Over his everyday uniform of patched corduroy pants, undershirt, and cigar stink, he had on an oversize ladies' pink plaid patchwork blazer (the kind with big shoulder pads, like Momma and her teacher friends wore when Daddy called them the "Monday-morning quarterbacks"). On his head, he wore a big white silk handkerchief with a dotted border; a necktie was knotted around his forehead. To really appreciate this scene, you should know that Mr. Nick had skin like Memaw's purse, with gray-black hair all over that looked like someone glued old SOS pads to him. Of the teeth you could see in the front of his mouth, one was gold and two were rotten. Whenever I thought of that troll under the bridge in the fairy tale, I thought of Mr. Nick.

All of us children had overheard the story of how Mr. Nick came to be at King's Way at one time or another, from our mothers telling our fathers or some other mother. The way I understood it, one Sunday morning Mr. and Mrs. Mounts had found Mr. Nick passed out drunk in their space in the church parking lot. People were beginning to arrive at church, so the Mountses made a loud and big deal of taking him inside the church, and then arranging for him to take a job as janitor in exchange for free room and board in the church basement. The Mountses got their Good Samaritan of the Year award, and that was that. Now and again, I would see Mr. Nick peeping around the sanctuary doorway during Sunday service. But neither the Mountses nor anyone else ever offered him a seat.

He just sort of faded into the background, and sometimes did a bad job of scraping the dried Play-Doh off our craft tables.

There he stood and there we sat, silent, all of us feeling ashamed somehow. Except for Mrs. Mounts, who put on her astonished face and said, "Oh look, children! It is the real Joseph in his coat-of-many-colors, come to judge our contest!"

Most of us just stayed openmouthed and not blinking, our crayons at a standstill. Meg rolled her eyes and put her head on the table. Then, from the back of the room, someone laughed. Two people joined in, then five. Mr. Nick just stared at the floor, like he knew he'd been tricked onto one of those Baptist trapdoors and he just wanted it to open up to get it over with.

"Now, children," Mrs. Mounts said. She was teetering on the edge of something herself and knew she had better get off fast. "Does anyone have any questions for Joseph?"

At that, Mr. Nick shot Mrs. Mounts a look that would have knocked me down. But she was much bigger.

Of course, Matt Keith had to raise his stupid hand.

"What happened to your hand, Joseph?" he asked. I could not tell whether Mrs. Mounts was relieved or frightened.

"Wellp," Mr. Nick said. Old country men seem to always end the word *well* with a *P.* He cleared his throat and fiddled with his pink silk blazer cuff. Once rolled up, it revealed a tattoo of a naked mermaid lady, with a big pink scar cutting across where her boobies ought to be, much to Mrs. Mounts's delight. "They say there ain't no way to get rid of a tattoo. But an AK-47 will take that sucker right off."

"Well, how nice!" Mrs. Mounts said, deciding to end the Q&A session she'd found so important a moment ago. "I guess we had better get on with our judging before Joseph has to hop back in his time machine!"

"Do you know Marty McFly? Is your time machine a De-Lorean?" Davy Marsh interrupted. "Because Teddy here wants to know."

This did not please Teddy, who looked as if he only kept from slapping Davy because it might break character and ruin the effect of his bathrobe. Mrs. Mounts was not happy, either, and she replied, serious as can be, "Davy, I certainly hope you are not referring to a PG-13 movie. We do not talk like that in church. I would not be surprised if Joseph did not go straight to Jesus when he got back and tell Him what you said. Now, Ni . . . er . . . Joseph . . . which one do you choose?"

Mr. Nick just continued to stand there as if he was waiting for instruction from the high authority and, like everyone else except for me, he had mistaken the high authority for Mrs. Mounts. She leaned over and whispered something in his ear, being careful not to get too close. Mr. Nick nodded and proclaimed, "Uh . . . now God done picked the winner already. I am just here to be the mouth . . . er . . . the tongue . . . of the God."

Mrs. Mounts slowly nodded approval.

"So, I reckon I'll pick that'n with the glitter stuck to his head," Mr. Nick continued, pointing toward Matt Keith with a dirty fingernail. Mrs. Mounts beamed from ear to ear. Naturally, all us kids were just as surprised as if we'd seen Lazarus raised from the dead. We gave halfhearted claps.

Mr. Nick turned to make a break for it during all the make-believe excitement, but Mrs. Mounts jerked him back by the elbow, then pulled her hand back just a little too quickly.

She was holding in her other hand one of those white Bibles kids get from the church when they are baptized, the kind that always has your name written in gold letters across the bottom (which is just a super way to spend church offering money in my opinion, since any kindergartner I know is simply devastated if his Bible is lost).

"On behalf of our Sunday School class, Joseph," Mrs. Mounts said, holding up that Bible like it was an Academy Award, "we present this gift of thanks for all your hard work . . . as Joseph. Will you do us the honor of reading our memory verse today? Please, I've marked it here for you. It would mean so much to the children."

Our whole little class head-bobbled and lied "yes" in unison.

Mr. Nick held open the pure white book, and the gold-trimmed pages looked like they might be tarnished with the soot on his hands. He squinted hard at the page but didn't say a word. Then he began to tremble. He looked around the room like one of us might dare get close enough to help him somehow, but no one did. Even Mrs. Mounts seemed to take a minuscule step back from him.

The quivering Bible tumbled out of his hands. Before it hit the ground at our leader's feet, he covered his eyes with his headscarf and ran out of the room.

Mrs. Mounts just stood there for a moment, then hocked up as big a smile as she could muster from the pit of her big old stomach. She picked up the dropped Bible and clutched it to her chest as if it were a bulletproof vest.

The other classes were being let out into the hall, so we all started to gather our papers and Popsicle-stick crosses. All the boys lined up to try on Matt's winning headdress, which Davy described as looking "like the Lebanon man with a machine gun" he'd seen on TV. All except for Teddy, that is, who just folded his towel neatly and walked out of the room with his chin down.

A week later, Teddy played Joseph in the drama by default, on account of every other boy in the class being afflicted with head lice.

THE RELIC OF SAINT MARGARET

There are a few key ingredients you need in order to build a Barbie diorama of a Catholic church—cracker boxes for the altar and the pews, of course; a bowl of water for the doorway and to dip babies in; and one chicken bone. This much I had gleaned from what creepy little hints my neighbor Mary Anna Stinson continued to drop about her church whenever Momma made me go over and try to play with her. Of course, Mary had not really meant that the bone should come from a chicken, but it was the best I could do, seeing as how I came from a good Baptist home, where we did not cut up our sainted loved ones and stick pieces of them in the altar.

I was sure Mary Anna was lying when she told me that Catholics did that, just as plain and simple as if she'd been telling me what was in her pencil box; but her mother, hemming Mary Anna's angel Halloween costume from the floor, had not even flinched as her daughter talked about that horror. She'd just kept right on, not missing so much as a stitch, while Mary Anna (who was not even allowed to come see *E. T.* with us because it was too violent) talked about how holy it was in her church to take an ax to your hero's limbs and then keep the bones around for good measure. These were called "relics."

It sounded like voodoo or something to me. And in fact,

before I'd even gotten out of the Stinsons' backyard that afternoon, I had prayed to Jesus and officially renounced my goal of becoming the world's first Baptist saint. I even told Him that if I were handcuffed one day and forced to become a Catholic, I would be sure to act as ornery as possible so that no one would mistake me for someone who was worthy to be dismembered. Jesus would understand.

But Mary Anna Stinson's tale would make for a good Halloween puppet play, I decided—one involving an unsaved Barbie dressed as the Wicked Witch of the West who tried to trick-or-treat at the door of a Catholic church, only to be scared away because all the people inside would do was throw water on her. I thought I would show the play to Daddy, and he would be so impressed with my growing knowledge of other faiths that he would let me put it on for the whole youth Sunday School Department.

But instead Daddy ruined the darn surprise by responding "What for?" when I asked him for his chicken bone from dinner. I knew in my heart that I wasn't plotting to misbehave in any way. But that "what for" let me know my game was up before it had even started.

"It's for the altar," I murmured, "for my cathedral. It was supposed to be a surprise."

Of course, Daddy said it would not be nice of me to put on a play like that; it would be making fun of people because of what they believed. People couldn't help what they believed, he said. Not Baptists, not Catholics, not anybody.

I tried not to pound the floor too loudly as I stomped away from the table. Daddy hadn't even looked up from his sermon notepad when he answered me, probably because he'd told me the thing about people not being able to help it about a hundred times already. He said I had to learn to be respectful of other faiths and I said I would try. That had been our Pastor–Daughter Responsive Reading for the month of October.

What I wanted to say was, *What about all the people who are going to burn alive because they don't believe in church at all? If it didn't matter, if nobody could help what they believed and what they didn't, and if faith was just a built-in thing, why do you bother with being a preacher at all?*

I stopped myself when my mind got to this point, because even I knew that I'd be stepping into blasphemy territory. That was far too easy to do when you were little and unknowing. (I was unusually learned, of course, but when it came to matters of potential sinning, I preferred to stay on the unlearned, I-don't-know-any-better side. It was always safer.)

Still, I couldn't get the whole matter of "relics" out of my mind. The thing that bothered me most about them, though I hated to admit it, was the fact that I was a little jealous of the faiths that had them. The little scroll that protected my classmate Bradley Reich's front door like a miniature lightsaber; the bones and chalices and shining statues of the Stinsons' church—all glass-encased pieces of old that must have stood out like magical pirate treasure above the dim, stuffy sanctuary. *What kid*, I asked my daddy, *what kid wouldn't want to believe in them?* If anything, they were a heck of a lot more inspirational to look at than the Christian Craft Display, which I supposed was the closest thing to a relics museum that our church had. This was put up about the first of October of every year, and was made up of things like a Nativity created out of salt dough, with the baby Jesus's head all pinched and Mary looking like she had dandruff all over.

Daddy just said that the Baptists did not have relics, and that was that. The Holy Spirit lived in people, not things. Even if the things were nicer and better looking than a lot of the people.

This made me ask, of course, before dinner was served one night and before my blood sugar had risen enough to help me shut my own mouth, whether some people could also be relics.

"What do you mean?" he asked.

"You know, part plain dead thing and part holy."

Daddy didn't miss the fact that as I asked the question, I was clearing the table of the craft project Momma had Meg and me working on all afternoon. We were making sachets to put into Mimi's drawers, so her clothes wouldn't have to smell so much like the hospital. Daddy didn't answer, because Momma had come back into the room with her casserole. But he gave me a look that said I'd better not dare say such a thing again. I didn't quite understand why, especially since my father had always said a church was on the wrong path when it became a sin for the members to ask questions. But he'd also said many times, low and sad, like a television doctor who was losing a patient on the table and knew the matter was out of his helpless hands, that when it came to certain things, and when it came to Mimi, our family was on its own to be its own church. No one else really understood our commandments or our burdens, and we really wouldn't wish baptism into the fold on anyone.

A few days later, Halloween came, and both the daylight and the weather turned topsy-turvy, throwing shadows through the front of our house at strange angles that God hadn't attempted for several months. It was His way of making us come inside together, Momma said, of making us look at one another in new ways again, to see what the summer had done. That Halloween,

Momma turned out to be right. Before the first week in November was over, God had managed to turn the light such that I could see a relic that had been under our roof all along.

Momma and I made the sacred discovery on the Sunday after Halloween. We'd just gotten back from Blessed Grove Baptist Church, where Daddy had served as special guest preacher for the weekend. Momma was in my room, gathering up my dirtied dresses and muttering something about how "if she'd only known," she would have dressed Meg and me in something a little plainer.

If she asked me, though, there was one thing that Blessed Grove Baptist did not need, and that was more *plain*. Not that it was supposed to matter, because Christians believe that church can be anywhere you make it, and you don't need stained glass or a marble baptistery to glorify the Lord. But still, Blessed Grove made me wonder just how decrepit a church had to be before it could be an official missions project of the Convention. I knew that those little pitiful hut-churches in Africa certainly qualified, and from what I could see, the place where I'd just attempted to be inspired was not much better.

We'd gotten there on Saturday night, and after going on a tour of the church with a lady in overalls, had gone to Big Boy to meet Blessed Grove's real pastor. He was wearing a uniform like a policeman, and Momma said this was because he had a whole other job, which was to be a prison guard up at the North Point Penitentiary. I wondered, though, if he'd just spent more of his time with the church, as God had probably meant for him to do, whether he wouldn't have been able to get pews that weren't propped up on the ends with stacks of newspapers, or real hymnals instead of photocopies that you had to share, or a steeple that didn't point sideways. When the waitress brought Meg the other half of her hamburger in a doggie bag at the end of the night, I half expected the man to ask if he could have it, to cut up the bun and use for Communion the next day. That is how sad it all was.

"Despite the circumstances, you girls were very nice and polite, and I appreciated that," Momma said as she put our dresses into the laundry basket. But when she lifted Meg's little plaid jumper, a scrap of folded paper fell out of the pocket.

"Hmmm . . . Meggie must've needed something to color on in church," Momma said, unfolding one of Blessed Grove's photocopied hymns. It was "Will There Be Any Stars in My Crown," the song selection I had always found to be the most regal of all the Baptist hymns. The writing was blurry and the paper smelled like Ditto machine ink. Plus, because Blessed Grove reused the papers over and over again, somebody's grocery list was written on the edge. (I wondered if someone who spelled *bread* with two *D*s really ever expected to attain any stars in any crown whatsoever.)

Momma turned out the rest of the pockets and let out a sigh.

"No tights here, of course. We'll need Sherlock himself to track down whatever happened to those. Emy, would you go ask your sister if she's still got her tights from today? I'm not buying one more pair, I swear I'm not . . ."

This had become something of a family joke, though Momma was laughing less and less about it. It started when Daddy told us that we each had to give our own sermons as we followed his guest preaching tours. Life sermons. We were to baptize each place with a little of our own spirits, maybe in the form of a nice compliment (preferably to someone who didn't deserve it, because as everyone knew but no one said, you got the highest rate of spiritual return on those), or a Bible verse recited, or a helping hand to the Sunday School teacher in cleaning up her classroom. Of course, Margaret Gates Hancock had chosen to make a more "real" contribution—my sister had left a trail of tights that stretched between every Baptist church in east Kentucky. These always seemed to miss the offering plate and usually wound up stuffed in a nursery trash can, as Meg's little legs swelled with the Sunday-morning mix of humidity and sanctity. On the rare occasion that some nursery sitter told her it wasn't proper to take off her clothes in the house of the Lord, Meg usually—silently—found a picture of Jesus, bare-legged and loinclothed, to point to on the wall. And that would be the end of that sermon.

Meg's door at the end of the hallway was closed, but for a crack. I could hear her bare feet padding around on the floor inside. And though I knew it was a sin to spy on people, unless you were their parents, I couldn't resist peeping for just a minute before I opened the door. Momma and Daddy never spied like this on Meg, that I knew about. I seemed to be the only one in the house who was fascinated by the fact that she kept her door closed sometimes. Truth be told, I was not nearly as concerned about what she might be doing in there as I was with the fact that she actually thought to close it. It had never even occurred to me to close my own bedroom door. That was something that adults and sometimes yelling teenagers on television did. Why part of my own flesh and blood would be born wanting to close it, I couldn't understand. Meg still seemed to like having a door between her and the rest of us. Sometimes I felt like the not-talking was only a part of it.

Boom. The door crack opened just wide enough for me to see, as something inside thumped against the ground. It was a foot—Meg's bare, stubby foot, to be exact—and it was pounding the hardwood in an awkward kind of dance, sort of like the kind I'd seen Momma do when she was watching her Jane Fonda on the VCR. Only Meg was sweatier than Momma ever was, and her face was redder. Not only that, but words were coming out of her mouth! She, who was supposedly barely able to babble!

I couldn't make out all of the words, because they seemed like a cross between shouts and notes—all frightening and raging and magnificent at the same time, like a cheerleader gone out of control. She held her baby blanket in her right hand, and punctuated the end of each (what seemed like a) sentence by thrusting it forward, toward the ground.

I crouched lower, and saw what she'd been aiming at. There, surrounding her feet in a semicircle, were Meg's stuffed animals. Big Bird sat with a baby doll, next to a collection of Happy Meal figures. To their right, what looked like Meg's remote-controlled KITT car and a pile of LEGO blocks had joined the congregation. Carefully laid out in front of each of them was a hymn sheet, lovingly smuggled from Blessed Grove Baptist by the first Christian daughter to have truly found a way to shoplift in the name of the Lord.

I wanted to roll on the floor. I wanted to laugh out loud and point and nearly wet my pants. But my heart seemed to have reverted back to its Sunday-morning-with-Daddy-at-the-height-of-the-pulpit pattern, a swift *beat-buh-beat* that meant only one thing.

It was rejoicing.

My little sister was a preacher. More than that, standing

there behind a pulpit made of a clothes hamper, with on-end-static hair electrified from the fast removal of her wool jumper, she was as beautiful and strange a werewolf as Thad Richards could ever dream of.

Meg concluded her sermon by shouting, three times, something that sounded like "God of Lamb!" I was pretty sure that the words didn't make any sense, but I got the feeling that that didn't matter to God, because she was just *too good*. I would have felt little prickles of jealousy had I not been in such holy awe. Then, when she asked everyone to pray, Big Bird *actually fell forward* onto his beak. I gasped out loud.

When I raised my head again (the way Meggie's eyes looked, I was afraid not to join in prayer), Meg was lifting up her newest toy, a small bear, and wrapping it up in her baby blanket, like the most precious object she owned.

She said, "I baptize you my brother, the name of the Father, Son, Holy Oat." Then she unwrapped the bear again and sat him in what appeared to be a sacred spot, right in front of the hamper-pulpit.

I could hear Momma turning the corner to come down the hall.

"Meg?" I pushed the door forward.

She groaned *hmmmm* and quickly sat on her hamper. As if it held some all-powerful secret that might escape.

I asked whether she had her tights, and when she said she didn't, I just nodded and left. I didn't go through her drawers, like Momma would have expected. I didn't ask if I could please play church, even though I wanted to. As I closed the door, I realized that for the rest of my life, part of loving my sister was going to mean forever being a spectator in the grand temple that she created around her, wherever she went. Sometimes it was a silent worship; other times, it was as loud and ornery as any black church magnified could ever hope to be. You weren't expected—or even allowed—to understand the Sister Bible. You just had to love it, and however frustrating that was, that was your lot.

About a month after I'd first witnessed my sister's private pulpit, Meg and I went on our first visit to the dentist. Meg was speaking more now, but strangers in general still got her trademarked sermon-with-the-eyes. Still, Dr. Kenton got a pretty good one. He was tall and dark-haired like Daddy, and I caught her batting her lashes once or twice; shouting *Aren't you just a doll!* with her lids when he offered to give her cherry-flavored fluoride.

But the sweet-eyes ended when Dr. Kenton met with us and Momma and Daddy in his office afterward. He brought up the subject of thumb-sucking, and said that Meg should be "weaned from it immediately" or her teeth were going to end up popping right out of the front of her lips, or something. Momma said that she didn't suck her thumb that often, and only when she was carrying her baby blanket around. Dr. Kenton waved his hand in the air like he was some brilliant magician, and said, "Well then, there we have it! Get rid of the blanket and the problem will probably go away. She's old enough anyway."

Now, at this bold order, I expected Daddy to stand up and flatten Dr. Kenton in his chair (with words only, of course). Where I came from, the local minister was the senior authority on who was old enough and too old for what. Mommas regularly lined up at the entrance to Daddy's study to consult on everything from the proper amount of eye shadow suitable for a sophomore in high school to whether five-year-olds might be confused for life by the inclusion of a menorah on an elementary school bulletin board.

But after all Daddy's work, checking and reversing the ages of his flock, he just nodded and smiled when Dr. Kenton declared that Meg was "too old" for a blanket. Momma and Daddy both took it like dumb little fools, and lowered their heads like wounded animals when he asked whether they had allowed me to "foster an overbite" for that long.

If I were Daddy, the last mention Dr. James Kenton would get in my life would be as an illustration in the next week's sermon about potential false prophets who might be hidden around the neighborhood. Nobody, nowhere, talked to my parents as if they knew "better." Except, of course, Jesus.

Strangely, the idea of giving up her blanket didn't seem to bother Meg that much. At least, not at first. In the car on the way home from the dentist, Momma offered up front to buy her a Care Bear in exchange for the old rag, and that seemed to settle it. (Of course, I, who had never sucked my thumb or relied on some moth-eaten relic for support, was offered no such free gift. I wondered if Momma had been talking to the speech teacher at school, who took three kids out of our class once a week and sent them back loaded with M&M's, all for pronouncing *fish* the right way. If you'd pronounced it the right way all along, you got squat. It was a cruel system.)

I didn't dare say anything about it being unfair, though. Especially not after Momma came to my room that evening and told me that she and Daddy had decided that Care Bears cost too much money. They were going to give Meg something that looked like a Care Bear, but wasn't, and wouldn't it be wonderful if I could display great faith and joy in the false bear? That way, it would surely spread to my dumb-as-dirt little sister, and she'd believe it was a Care Bear, too.

I said that I would obey. But that was before I went to go get Meg from her room for dinner; before I arrived at her doorway, cracked open again, and saw that she was once again deep into church. Only this was another, more private type of service. A funeral.

Meggie sat kneeling beside her little bed, her head down on her arms in front of her. Little moans came from a place so deep that I knew I would never be able to reach it myself, even with the most fervent prayer I ever mustered.

Slowly, she picked up the little baby blanket that was laid out in front of her and folded it as gently as her chubby hands could, almost as if she were getting ready to lay down her only child to rest.

Suddenly I was angry. By making her just give up the blanket she'd trusted like a savior and shield since birth, Momma and Daddy were making Meg do what Daddy had claimed Baptists and Catholics and all religious people alike *couldn't* do—turn off their belief in something like they were flicking a switch.

After dinner, when Momma presented Meg with the fake Care Bear (which was actually not even a bear at all, but some kind of pink possum-like thing with a giant head and a long tail), I was almost too upset to think about dessert. Meggie smiled and clapped—a little halfheartedly, I thought—while Daddy showed her different tricks that the Thing's tail could do.

Would you do it again? I wanted to ask him. *Would you go into the Stinsons' cathedral on Sunday morning and take their saint-finger-bones out of the altar, and then replace them with Lincoln Logs and say, "Well, there you go! It's exactly the same thing! Y'all just carry on worshipping!"*

Who knows, maybe he would, in front of a cathedral of adults. Maybe it got easier to flip the belief switch as you grew, and Meg and I just didn't know.

As it turned out, though, Meg didn't have to find out right then. About a week later, when Meg had retired the Thing to the bottom of the toy box with a broken tail, the Blanket reappeared. Meg ran to the breakfast table, holding it high and bright ahead of her like a guiding star. Momma and Daddy both said they had no idea how it had gotten into her bed. I even heard them arguing about who had done it as they cleared the dishes, and neither would admit it.

But the Blanket never left Meg Hancock's side again. Every night, she put it across the top of her pillow before she said her prayers, and it stayed there until the morning. All through her sleep, I imagined that my sister's dreams made their way into its fibers, in between the faint images of puppy dogs and outlines of old tears. What she dreamed of, what she believed in, healed up the holes.

Yes, it's true, Daddy kept on telling me, that Baptists didn't believe in *things*. That true believers didn't worship stuff. But I couldn't help but wonder if off in some remote corner of heaven, past the sanctuary of the grandparents and farther on even than the corner for the pets, there was a special cloud set aside. Strewn with tattered blankets, stuffed animals with the eyes missing, and capes from costumes long since forgotten.

It was there to accept the prayers of the very young.

Lesson 4

Momma and
Aunt Kit

My winning
bride costume

faithfulness

THE PAGAN FROG PIN OF GENERAL DRIVE

Sometimes the most confusing part of being a Christian is keeping track of all God's different jobs. There is the Merciful God and the Vengeful God, the Loving God and the Awesome God (the older kids in the youth group liked Him), the Ultimate Judge and the Great Physician, and the Great I Am (and I couldn't ever figure out what that last one meant for the life of me). Sometimes when I sat in GAs and tried to list out all God's different brands of goodness, I envied my Catholic neighbor Mary Anna, who, as far as I could tell, had a God who wore only two hats—He was a physician and a chef. He could heal people and He could turn Himself into bread, and that was it. That was all you needed to know.

We Baptist kids didn't have it so easy. So, though I knew it set me three sins back from atonement to think of Him this way, I kept God's duties straight in my head by picturing Him as a giant Barbie doll, except with hairy legs and sandals. His face never changed, but His careers and His outfits did so long as your little fingers and little prayers worked fast enough.

But the task was twice as hard for me than for the other kids, because I received the Word from a minister who wore more than one hat, too. Daddy had a sermon voice and an at-home voice; his church smiles and his at-home grins; his damnation-from-above tone, and his damnation-on-whoever-flooded-the-bathroom-floor-trying-to-play-Olympics tone. He had his good suit and he had his blue jeans.

Now, for the other kids in my Sunday School class, the fact that my Daddy wore blue jeans at all seemed to be the hardest thing to reconcile in their minds. Whenever one of them saw us in the grocery store on a Saturday, me in my shorts and Daddy in his Wranglers, they always staggered backward, as if they were looking at Daddy with no pants on at all. I might have just blamed this on the fact that they were my age, and not all kids my age could be expected to know how to behave properly around an elder. But from what I saw, their mommas weren't much better. When their carts bumped Daddy's accidentally, some of them got real flushed and embarrassed. They tried oh-so-casually to throw coats over their carts, which happened to contain cartons of cigarettes and the occasional wine cooler. And then they said things like, "Why, Reverend Hancock, you shop here at this grocery?"

No ma'am, I always bit my tongue to keep from saying. *No, we don't shop at the grocery. Manna usually just falls out of the sky at our house.*

The funniest part of all was, I felt like I was as dumb as dirt as any of them when it came to figuring out how the sweet, perfect voice of the Almighty fit into the same voice box with snores so godawful that Momma sometimes slept in my room. Me, of all children, should have gotten some close-up glimpse of where angel's wing met ordinary Daddy's backbone.

But by the middle of my second-grade year—early into cursive, half past the multiplication tables, and just four GA patches short of achieving total enlightenment—I still hadn't figured out how he worked. Or was it, how *He* worked?

Once, I thought I was close. My classmate Nicole held

a church children's "Harvest Party" (this is Baptist code for "Halloween Party") out on her farm, and as my grand prize for prettiest costume (I was a bride, and wore Suzanne's old flower-girl dress, which the year before had been an angel's robe, and the year before that, the bottom to my lamb outfit. I had thus completed the trinity of Halloween characters that it was acceptable for a good Christian girl to wear), I won a little plastic pin. It was shaped like a frog wearing a wizard's cap with a tiny star on it, and it was attached to a piece of cardboard that read LUCKY PIN in glittery silver script.

Nicole's mother was mortified that I was the one who won that pin. She tried to get me to exchange it for a dollar from her purse, and when I said I would rather keep the pin, she made me promise to tell my parents that the frog was really some sort of a spacefrog or scientist frog, and that was why he had on the cap with a star on it. I wasn't to say anything about it being a magical frog or wizard frog or anything pagan-like, because it most certainly *was not*. I just nodded politely as Nicole's momma waved me out of the driveway that evening, her fingers shaking and her face blushing.

I didn't care what Nicole's momma wanted me to call the pin; I only cared about what I wanted to do with it. That pin was going to be the first-ever just-because gift that I'd ever given to anyone. It wasn't a holiday, it wasn't a birthday. And it wasn't anything I'd glopped together on behalf of a teacher who'd ordered me to express generosity through balsa wood and tempera paint. I knew, from the moment it entered my hand in victory, that I was going to give that frog pin to Daddy.

In the car on the way home, I didn't take my eyes off the

pin. Every time Momma hit a bump in the back roads that stretched between our home and the many wily paths of our congregants, I straightened it again on its cardboard backing. It was a strange new feeling, truly wanting someone else to have something that I'd earned outright. I wanted to tell Momma about it as she drove, but I thought better of it. If she knew that this was the first time the true spirit of giving had ever hit me, she might make me go back and complete all of Vacation Bible School, starting with the nursery level. And besides, I did not want to crush her spirit to pieces when she realized I had chosen to give my only-begotten frog pin to my father.

Of course, there was another motive behind the gift—not a sinful one, of course, because it did not entail taking anything from Daddy. It just meant finally getting what I was rightfully entitled to by virtue of being his daughter. I wanted to see how the Word of God worked in and through him. I wanted to know where the hidden touchstone was inside our house that allowed him to make the change, that turned his hands from those that dipped Meg, kicking and screaming, into the bathtub at night, to hands that could cleanse souls and reset spirits with a single dip in holier waters. I wanted to know how he could make his old church softball cap look like a halo to Mrs. Mounts. I wanted, just for a moment, to feel the same reverence as the congregants who brought gifts of homemade honey and jam to our front door, as thanks to Daddy for saving their very souls. Those people never stayed long enough to see Daddy mow the lawn in his dirty undershirt. I always had to. And darn it if it wasn't my turn to stand amazed.

As we made our way toward home that night, I rehearsed the pin-giving in my head. After carefully wrapping the pin in a Kleenex tissue (one of the peach ones from the down-stairs guest bathroom, since they looked the most like wrapping paper, and I couldn't ask Momma for the real stuff), I'd go up to my father as he had his nightly quiet time in the den. Once I was sure we were alone, I'd quietly, reverently, present it to him.

This is a lucky frog, I'd say. I'd tell him that he could take it with him, to help and protect him when he traveled for missions work.

And then, after a quick check of all the doorways to make sure Momma and Meg weren't listening, he'd tell me the truth.

I don't need a luck charm, he'd say. *I have a far greater secret, and here it is. It is not just the love of God, because everyone at church has that, and people don't just bow their heads for everyone, do they? Here's the key to why everyone just bows when I say so. Here's why when I tell people they're married, they believe me, and no one believes you and Meg when you take my wedding script and offer to marry people in the backyard for a quarter. Here's how I understand what God is saying when other people don't. And most important, here's how I can spank your legs while telling all the other church parents to "suffer the little children."*

And then it would happen. He would tell me the secret to his holiness, whatever it was, and I would know how it all worked. Then I, daughter of the Most High of General Drive, would have knowledge of her rightful place in the kingdom. The fatherdom.

I felt like I was being terribly audacious, walking up to Daddy at that just-before-my-bedtime time of day, the hour that Momma always referred to, whispering and shooing me out of the room with a tap on the rear end, as "his quiet time."

Even though Daddy was always preaching that his door was *always* open to his dear congregation. I chose to believe this wasn't a lie, even though Meg and I were valid members of his flock, too. I just thought it was his way of making sure that no daughter of his disgraced the Lord's business by discussing it in footy pajamas. After all, it was an important Christian truth that only the brightest of white pinafores and largest of hats could be seen from heaven.

But still, I told myself, zipping up the front of my footy jumpsuit as I said a silent prayer, this was an exceptional case.

As humbly and reverently as possible, and checking twice over my shoulder to make sure Momma was still occupied in the other room (fighting tooth and nail to make Meg take off her sneakers before getting into bed), I padded across our den floor to where Daddy sat. This was the sacred "quiet time," all right, and everything in my little body recognized it. I felt a flush of heat start to creep around the elastic in my cuffs. The puddle of light from Daddy's reading lamp might as well have been a force field; that Clive Cussler novel was a shield above his heart. I couldn't help but think of the marine sergeant who had come to address my Sunday School class on Patriotic Sunday the year before. He'd said that a soldier became a different person when he put on his uniform; he couldn't really think of his home or his wife or his little girls. Having never really spoken to my father this late at night, and never in his quiet-time bathrobe, I wondered whether he could even recognize me. Was he just another soldier in his midnight relief fatigues—off duty, but on watch?

"Miss Em? Shouldn't you be in bed?" Daddy spoke without even looking up to see me.

Well, that settled that.

"I . . . ," I fumbled. "Momma couldn't tuck me in. I mean *yet*, she couldn't tuck me in yet. Because of Meg and what Meg is doing."

I added that last part quickly. More quickly than I expected, because a new feeling had crept into the room behind me as I stood before my father. Was I *nervous*? *Me*, in front of *Daddy*? And was this how everyone in our congregation must *always* feel when they talked to him? When they were dressed in their finest, and their questions were of the highest spiritual order, in their hearts did they all have on footy jammies?

The thought made me feel better somehow, and I stepped forward and placed the little Kleenex-wrapped bundle on his knee.

Then I stood back and waited. I exhaled and I prayed and I waited for it to all be worth it; for Daddy to tell me that he didn't need a pin to protect him on his missions work, because he had a God-given power to be Clark Kent and Super Saver all at once. And here was exactly how it worked—

"Well, thank you, kid!" Daddy suddenly shouted, shattering the moment with his attempt at a Howdy Doody accent. "Ain't that finer 'n a frog hair. Well, come to think of it, it *is* a frog hair!"

And that time, he did actually look up at me. But dear Lord, how I wished he hadn't.

When I looked up, Daddy was holding the pin at eye level, making it dance back and forth across his nose. There was no reverent stare; no sign that he was ready to share with me the source of his true magic. There was no sign of any magic whatsoever, unless you figured God's will somehow played into the toe of my pajama splitting open at that precise moment.

I managed a grin, finally. I knew that Daddy wouldn't let that frog pin stop its pagan dancing until I did.

He told me that he was going to pin the frog to his bathrobe, and take the bathrobe with him every time he traveled.

"That way," he said, in the same tone of voice he used to tell the preschoolers how God created the world, using about five words and making dumb faces, "I'll always be protected by Mr. Magic Frog, wherever I go! A good travelin' preacher needs that sometimes."

And then he winked. Not a passing-of-the-sacred-knowledge kind of wink, but an I've-got-your-nose kind. It was pathetic.

I didn't quite know what to say, so I nodded and mumbled something about needing to get to bed. Before I'd reached the end of the den, I almost turned back to tell Daddy good night once again, but I couldn't. I knew that every time I saw him pack that bathrobe for a mission trip, one where he apparently counted the protections of a plastic frog among the tools in his spiritual arsenal, he'd seem just a little less holy-mysterious in my eyes.

When Momma tucked me in that night, I told her I had outgrown footy pajamas.

THE CRAYON-WRITING ON THE WALL

Damascus, the magical little town in the Kentucky foothills where Momma and Aunt Kit grew up, had been originally settled by angels, Kit once told me. That was the only way you could explain how anyone ever got to that spot—roads didn't wind there naturally; they had to be cut in and through the edges of the limestone bowl that cradled Damascus like a sacred child. So it only made sense that those who originally found it flew in from above, and their sweetness collected into the little lake at the town's center, seeping into the veins and skins of the most blessed families you could ever hope to know. There was proof of this history, Kit said, in the bridge that led us across the town line. Instead of bumping and mumbling along, the Damascus Creek bridge seemed to sing whenever we crossed it, as if some spirit of the land itself would welcome us every Labor Day weekend of my Bluegrass childhood.

But as soon as we got into town, usually on a Sunday afternoon, everything would be silent again. This was because Damascus was, as Momma said, "one of the last true godly places on earth." That meant that, with the exception of the one hour that Gardenia Bakery opened up its doors after church, to provide everyone with their supply of Lord's Day yeast rolls, all of Damascus was closed and reverent on Sundays.

It was as peaceful and pleasant as all my winter dreams, when I went there and felt the sunshine through the oaks.

By the Labor Day of my tenth year, I had been to Damascus more summers than I could remember, and its memory had kept me warm through more winters than I could count. But in all my dreams, I had somehow forgotten just how gosh-awful and rocky the trip there with my cousins could be. And that year was the worst.

You see, as pretty as the country drive was, romantic thoughts, and even common decency, were difficult to maintain in the Hancock Family Station Wagon. This was especially true when that wagon was chock-full of our own most unholy, and most fun, relatives—Momma's sister Kit, and her three kids, Suzanne, Clayton, and Dottie Jane.

Now, if you were in this car, you would thank me for listing everyone's name and vitals individually, because to look at us all there, we seemed just like my doll drawer at home—arms and legs all jumbled up together and thrown here and there till you couldn't tell what belonged to who. Baby Clayton, who was nearly two and finally sleeping, was in the middle in his car seat. Suzanne, who was almost fourteen and almost too cool for me, was turned with her back resting against the driver's seat, legs thrown over the backseat bench just to the point where they would interfere with Dottie Jane's ability to sit the way she wanted. Dottie Jane was just a year younger than me then, but people always thought she was closer to Meg's age on account of the itty-bitty body she got from her daddy's momma.

Meg had cheeseburger foil wrapped around her head and was gripping the back window ledge, pretending she had to shoot out all enemy tractors. And in the middle of it all, of course, you could still find the good Elizabeth Hancock, behind Momma, seat belt buckled.

"Chain chain *chaaaaaain* . . . !" Aunt Kit hollered out the window at the prison work crew hacking at the side of the road. This made Momma nearly swerve into a ditch, but she got control back as usual. Meg and I were never quite sure of the momma we were going to get when Kit was around. Half the time she was hollering, too, but the other half she went into teacher mode as if she were the prom chaperone at Rowdy Child High School.

"Kit!" Momma shouted, swallowing a laugh. In my mind, I bet she had to stop herself from reaching around her neck for a whistle that wasn't there. "You are going to make the state troopers pull us over any minute, and with all these rascals not in seat belts they will haul me right in. And it'll be me out there shoveling rocks, do you hear me? Now, if everyone could just try to settle down and get themselves together, we are almost there. *Almost there.*"

Momma pointed a finger at us through the rearview mirror for emphasis, and caught sight of a particularly messy roadtrip casualty. "Oh Lord. Oh Kit, you're gonna have to get a start on Clayton. There are baby wipes in the backseat pocket. Emy, you help her. Here, Kit, take a look."

Momma turned the rearview mirror so Kit could get a full-on glance.

Now, in a summertime vacation car, a kid really gets to experience the kind of squalor she is asked to thank God daily that she does not live in. It was dream-like in its own way for my cousins and Meg and me, because any other place we ate and slept, any other time of year, our mommas simply would not have allowed such conditions. But summertime made hypocrites out of all parents. It made them overlook the presence of stale Happy Meal french fries that had found their way into every seat crevice and cranny. It made them ignore the smell of Meg's untouched hamburger from the night before, which she shoved under the driver's seat in order to get dessert. It made them blind to melted crayons on window ledges and piles of wadded-up pages of gas station "mystery pen" fun booklets. And of course, it rendered them too sun-lazy to dust off the powdery residue of Pixy Stix that clung to everything, evidence of a nutritional assault that Dr. Spock would smite any parent for inflicting. During the school year, that is.

In the middle of it all that day sat the crown jewel, the family's only little boy, asleep in the pool of melted chocolate Dairy Queen Buster Bar that had flooded his car seat.

Aunt Kit was barely getting out words in between spasms of laughter so hard they didn't make any sound. "Oh, Sharon, look! He's even gotten it in his hair! Clay? Clayton, honey, wake up."

Now we were all laughing, even Momma. She was still trying to be the Head Mom in Charge, though. Trying. "Oh, I'm looking, Kit, believe you me. And I can't wait for the look my mother-in-law will give me when she sees this. She already thinks I've turned Meg masculine . . ."

Momma was referring to an incident that had occurred the December before, in which Meg went to sleep with a mouthful of Big League Chew at the church kindergarten lock-in, and woke up the next day with her head stuck to the vestibule carpet. Momma's solution was to get it all chopped out and have Meg's hair cut short. Meg loved this, because it made her look like Mary Lou Retton. Memaw threw a fit and said it made her look like Paul McCartney. And you did not get Memaw going on the Beatles, whom she said started the downfall of Baptist youth everywhere.

Momma stopped herself and let out a sigh, out of breath, and out of strength to stop the force of a hidden spirit that pushed on her insides with every cackle and holler that we made. I knew that with her next breath, she would be able to stand it no longer and full possession would take place.

I knew "possession," Daddy said, was really something made up. But every time I was with my aunt and cousins, I would swear before the Lord that I saw it happen. It was not as if something that was completely outside of us got in there and took over; it was when something little teeny-tiny in all of us that was hidden the rest of the time suddenly got so big and blown up that it exploded. It was what I called miraculous magnification of the spirit, and it could really happen in any group of people. When you were with a mean crowd, your meanness got magnified. In an excited crowd, like backstage before a ballet recital, your heart would get to beating so hard in time with everyone else's that you were shocked the audience couldn't hear it. Those were the common things to get magnified.

But there was another spirit, rare as ball lightning, that could get blown up at very special times. In fact, it was the subject of my fourth-grade science project (for which I received a D from Miss Coker, who only gave A's to the really poor kids anyhow, seeing as how they had to overcome so much more than me in order to make mold grow on bread).

My theory was that deep in the human anatomy, in the organ that is our soul, where God and the Devil each have a hand resting at all times, sometimes their fingers touch by accident. This makes the Spark, a short and brilliant lightning like a firefly makes, powered by just the right mix of purest joy and most fiery mischief. And like a firefly, it is usually gone so quickly you don't even see it, unless there are other fireflies around. And they set off one another's Sparks, one after the other again and again until the air is electric.

Right then, Aunt Kit's electric Spark was strong enough to draw Momma's, too long hidden, right out of her.

Momma took a deep breath to speak. ". . . and now, my own sister has gone and baptized our family's only son with hot fudge."

Aunt Kit threw her head back and tossed her laugh out the sunroof, into the open farm country where all laughs are free to expand back to their natural sizes. Momma smiled and looked at Kit and then back at all of us, and for just a moment, I saw the Spark. Right at the corner of her eye. It was beautiful and bright, but it was only the beginning.

The true miracle didn't happen until the customary first event of the weekend—the "replace-the-wreaths" trip Momma and Aunt Kit made us take to Damascus Cemetery, where their daddy and grandparents were buried.

Now, though we felt horribly guilty about it, my cousins and I had not ever been able to get worked up with sadness over the cemetery trip. We'd barely known our great-grandparents, and Momma and Kit's daddy had gone up to be with Jesus long before we were born.

But that did not mean Emy Hancock was not rightfully

reverent about the trip, oh no! I knew, just to look at it, that the Damascus Cemetery was extra sacred—like Momma said, it was the very spot on earth where God planted the best of his angels. It was not wretched and horrible like all the other graveyards I had heard about, with tombstones all covered with cobwebs and bony hands sticking up out of the ground. I can still remember, before our first visit, Momma telling us that "the only things in Damascus Cemetery that will bring tears of horror to your eyes are those plastic swans the Gooches put out to glorify the memory of their loved ones."

Now, this particular Labor Day weekend, everyone must have had better things to do than hang out with dead relatives, because Damascus Cemetery was completely empty, so to speak. But clouds were gathering overhead, and the humidity made the air the kind you could run around buck naked in and still feel covered head-to-toe. Looking back, I remember feeling an electricity trying to form in the sticky mist. It was a charge that seemed out of place—almost dangerous, considering where we were. And that, combined with the charges brought out by being around one another, already almost visible jumping from body to body in the setting sun, made me both excited and wary for what the evening might hold. Something about cemeteries, just like churches and just like all places where Jesus walks, made them wonderfully happy playgrounds when the adults who thought they owned them were not around. And Momma and Aunt Kit were not like those adults. Maybe when they were apart, but never when they were together.

When we got through the big iron gates, down the narrow road lined with daffodils placed by the American Legion Auxiliary, Momma started driving slower than molasses. Of course, part of the reason was out of politeness to the dead people. But there was something else that always slowed her down, something I was never able to figure out. Every year, every time she and Kit got the Volvo closer to their daddy's grave, they seemed to play lost. One of them would always shake her head and say, "Well, I can never find this thing for the life of me," and the other would laugh and say, "I know, I know, and we've done this a hundred times." I recognized the game because I had played it a hundred times myself, when I couldn't find my hairbrush for Momma after a swim in the pool, or the way to the GA room at church.

Momma finally parked in her usual spot, just off the road under a big dogwood.

Suzanne, Meg, and Dottie Jane darted out of the car immediately, off to watch Meg make good on her bet to knock on the door of an old mausoleum. Suzanne had offered to up the ante by making Meg say some spell she and Dottie Jane heard on *Raiders of the Lost Ark*. I knew that this was just Suzanne's way of rubbing it in to Meg and me that she and Dottie Jane had HBO and got to watch whenever they wanted. This was a sore subject with me, Suzanne knew, because putting on plays for the family that I wrote used to be our main form of entertainment at these reunions of ours. It all stopped, though, when Suzanne and Dottie Jane's babysitter let us watch this HBO special about girls who got money for dancing on a pole all night wearing metal bras. When my next family drama included all of us dancing across Aunt Kit's wet bar wearing aluminum foil, Momma had called a halt to the cable TV. If you ask me, the whole thing was due to the almighty power of the ignited Spark, and all God-given fireworks happen for a reason that is not ours to question.

Anyhow, I stayed behind and helped Momma and Kit with the big potted yellow mums and marigolds. I told them I did not care to be a part of the mausoleum prank, mainly because it was disrespectful to the dead. But also because a child blessed with a fertile imagination such as mine had to use it wisely and temper it with mercy on herself, and I knew better than to let my mind play ding-dong-ditch at twilight with a bunch of rotting zombies. I kept this fear to myself, though, because being scared of dying is one of the most sinfully un-Christian things you can do.

"Ah-ah! Y'all get back here, right now!" Aunt Kit shouted at the crew headed for the mausoleum. "Aunt Sharon and I need to show you something. It will only take a minute."

They led us all to the west side of the cemetery in a lineup that went from big to little, with Meg trailing at the back. (She had taken to wearing this one pair of Kanga-ROOS sneakers that she had long since outgrown, and was splitting out of. Momma had finally given up and told her to go ahead and wear them till they cut off her circulation and she got crippled for life.) We went directly to a little corner plot where the grass had been just mowed by a different mower and in a different shape than whatever had cut the rest of the cemetery lawn. Someone hadn't wanted the big cemetery tractor-mower to move and shake over this shady spot of earth. I was curious to see just why, until we finally got close enough to it. Then, oh how I wished I had just run off with the rest to the mausoleum, too fast and too far for Momma and Kit to have called me back. For what I saw, what my own mother in all her meanness had actually made me look at, chilled me in the heat like an Africa malaria victim.

The grave had a little tiny picket fence around it, just like Grandy used around his tomato patch. There was a little angel with a bowed head and praying hands, who could never fly on account of being made of concrete. A pink-and-white stuffed bunny—the kind Dottie Jane would have ordinarily snatched up in a second for her collection—stared up at us unafraid and undisturbed from the ground. And on the stone itself, the most creepy-as-all-get-out thing that any grave can have, was the photograph of a smiling blue-eyed girl in her Easter dress and hat. Her face was mounted up there permanently behind Plexiglas, just like someone had wanted a sign there saying, PLEASE COMPARE WHAT KATIE LOU LITTLE, AGE 7, USED TO LOOK LIKE, WITH WHAT YOU KNOW IN YOUR AWFUL IMAGINATION SHE MOST DEFINITELY DOES NOT LOOK LIKE BY NOW. Strangest of all was the newness and cleanness of everything, as if someone had just been there fixing and planting and grooming. The date of death on the stone was 1952.

Suddenly my mind could see her, the one who put up the picket fence and fixed the little grass blades and tied the little pink bows. She was a little momma exactly like my own little momma. A momma who couldn't seem to stop combing little hair.

"Now," Momma said, almost at a whisper. She patted Meg's head. "This little girl . . . this little girl lived across the street from Aunt Kit and me when we were little. And she was playing near the street and not looking both ways one day, and a car hit her. And she died."

We were all silent, except for Suzanne, who kept letting out loud huffs and looking at her Swatch.

"Okay, guys, we get it," Suzanne said, "don't play in the street blah blah blah. Can we please go now?"

I couldn't believe she could look Katie Lou Little in the eye and say those words.

"Yeah, yeah, go on," Kit said. "But no running, and do *not* scream."

Suzanne turned and walked away without a pause, as if she had just been waiting in line for fast food. Meg and Dottie Jane followed, heads down, at a slower pace than Suzanne at first, then quickening as they got farther and farther from the grave site. I did not move. Momma knelt beside me and did my favorite Momma comfort skill, putting her hand on the small of my back.

"Em? You okay?" she whispered. A little breeze blew between her hair and mine and seemed to pat both our shoulders.

"I just don't understand one thing," I told her. "Katie Lou is holding a white Bible in that picture. She must have gone to church."

"Well, yes, I guess so. Her dress was pretty, wasn't it?"

"Then how?" I said. "How come she wasn't protected, from the car and all? Was she not a Baptist?"

"I don't know, honey. I don't know. Are you sad? You want to go sit in the car until we're done here?"

"No, I'm fine. I was just thinking about Mrs. Mounts. She thinks saying 'I don't know' about anything that has to do with dying and God and heaven is just faithlessness. I am going to save that question about Katie and the car for her and hope that it gets her good."

Momma smiled. She combed my hair with her fingers. "Just don't sass, but you go right ahead. Now, do you want to run along and play with the riffraff, Princess Emy?"

"No. I think I want to walk by myself."

She let me go with the promise that I wouldn't walk too far, shouting out behind me, "And Emy! You are *not* to redistribute the flowers to the graves that don't have any, you hear me?"

I pretended not to. If you asked me, one of the biggest lies ever told in church was the one about death being "the great equalizer." I had heard it said often, in sermons that my daddy didn't preach, that we didn't *have* to worry about who had what after we were dead, because all Christ's children are one and the same when they rise to meet Him. Well, if that was the truth, then all the dead in the Damascus Cemetery were just too darn lazy to move it on up. Here, he who was a big-time name in life was *still* a big-time name, plain for all to see forever, in the strongest marble. And he who never was, was just a few faded letters half crumbled away in cheap, moss-ridden concrete.

As big and rolling as the grounds were, from wherever I walked in the cemetery that day, I could always see the few big, spotlighted obelisks, engraved with names like CLAY, WALKER, and BOONE, names I had seen before in Damascus, on schools, baseball outfield billboards, and the new hospital. But these monuments were not thrilling to look at. Up close, they were just big hulks with no personality or good story to tell.

So I walked farther, to the area out by the cemetery's edge, near the cow pasture, where just a twisted old barbed-wire fence separated the bodies from the manure. This was, as Momma told me, what used to be the black people corner of the cemetery, but had been just the poor people corner for a long time. This was the place I both hated to look at and was magnetically drawn to, just like the sight of Pepsi Moffett when she wore an old ratty pair of tennis shoes with her dress to school awards day. Here some of the graves looked homemade, decorated with wood-burning kits or the kind of five-cent metal numbers you stick on mailboxes. Some weren't even spelled correctly. I couldn't help but think that most of the people buried here were probably too poor and ignorant to go to church and be baptized. They couldn't be allowed into the kingdom of heaven, so their last and greatest glory had to be someone's old lawn ornament or wood-shop project. I felt their heavy pitifulness and wanted to run, to get away from the embarrassment that was both theirs and mine.

A voice interrupted my thoughts.

"Emy! Get out of there!"

It was Suzanne.

"C'mon, you've been *here*? This is the poor part! We saw one grave way over there with this awesome train made out of bronze laid out across the top, and you completely missed it! Didn't she, Dot? It had to have cost like ten thousand bucks, didn't it?"

Dottie Jane didn't answer. She was more fascinated with a plastic flower she'd picked off a nearby plain white wooden cross. She held it to her nose and made a sour face. "This just reeks of Kmart." (Now, I liked to think I was good at just about everything, but one talent I had found on this earth that was purely Dottie Jane was the ability to track a scent better than an old coonhound. Dottie Jane smelled everything, everywhere we went. One year at our family Christmas Eve get-together, this skill got Dottie Jane exiled to the guest bedroom for an hour, after she announced that the sweater Uncle Ron gave her in a Gap box actually had the odor of Sam's Club.) Now she picked up an old rain-faded plastic doll, also left at the foot of the cross. Its head fell off, and this was somehow just as disgusting to Dottie Jane as if she had picked up a real decapitated human being.

"Look, Suzanne, it's not even a real Barbie! Ewww!" she shouted, laughing and holding the doll at arm's length.

"Ewww, put that down, Dot! Don't touch anything. Emy, you can be so creepy. Why are you wandering over here?" Suzanne yelled.

"Hey!" Meg suddenly spoke up. "Let's get crayons and paper from the car and make rubbings. For the collection."

The rubbings collection was the one thing owned and respected in common among all us cousins. It had started as a project to keep us all occupied one evening at the hospital, when my grandmother Mimi first went into her coma. Momma had given the idea to us, and I think she got it out of one of her teacher books. The game was, you had to go around putting notebook paper over some surface, and then scratching the relief with a crayon. Then, you had to bring your finding back to the group, and everyone had to take turns guessing which surface had made the pattern. If you couldn't guess, you had to come up with some good story about what it might be. Of course, I had the best stories, and so everyone had become turned on to the game. Since then, we had expanded it, taking samples of rubbings from every spot we visited, together and apart—license plates at gas stations in Tennessee; the Braille menu Meg acquired on a dare at a Carolina McDonald's; the cobblestone walkway from the Southern Baptist Convention in New Orleans.

Of course, the headstones at Damascus Cemetery promised both quality textures and good story fodder. Suzanne volunteered to sneak to the car to get supplies without disturbing our mothers, who were now staring arm in arm at their grandparents' grave. Cousin in Chief as always, she directed us all to a rich-looking section of the cemetery, somewhere midway between the immortally extravagant and the damned pitiful. I complied, as only the sharp marble engravings promised clear reliefs. I was ready for relief, too, from the section of sad cement.

But something worse loomed for me: the revelation that it took more than money to make one's name immortal in Damascus Cemetery.

"Why's this lady not have any name?" Dottie Jane said, sniffing out what was not right a split second before the rest of us. She was pointing at a huge block of a tombstone, twice as big as a refrigerator box and gilded with heavy bronzed letters that spelled out ROBERT COLEMAN PRESTON. Right below it, carved into the stone in much smaller script, was AND HIS BELOVED WIFE. That was it. Whoever the lady was, she hadn't been there long. The date said that she'd passed away not many years before, right after her husband. And in the matter of just a few summers, she had been reduced to less than a name. Sure, it was spelled out in full down on the footstone, down where only the cemetery man who had to mow around it would bother to look. The glory part of the monument was just for Robert Coleman Preston—Church Deacon, Shriner, and President, Farmer's Bank of Damascus.

"I think Mom knows them," Suzanne said. "I think I've heard her talk about them, giving pool parties for the teenagers at church. They were just these old people who liked throwing birthday parties for every kid at the church, whether they knew them or not. I don't think they even had kids of their own, but they threw all these birthday parties. I think her name was maybe Mable or something. Isn't that a bizarre story?"

I hadn't known Mrs. Preston, but something in me began to hurt for her. Slowly, I could see the grass melting away before my feet, revealing a woman lying lonely and still, holding in her lap a birthday cake with someone else's name on it. It *was* a little bizarre. But as much as I respected God's law of dead people becoming spirits, it just seemed as though she— whoever she was—must have had enough life in her to keep from turning invisible and no-name so fast.

She was not alone in fading, though. If you looked, many of the surrounding headstones simply read WIFE or MOTHER. We read them in silence, not saying a word but exchanging electric currents, fueled this time by a collective anger and confusion that jumped within and among us. *Was this what our mothers had meant by "angels" in Damascus? That it was a place that eventually turned all mommas, even all wannabe mommas, invisible? And if they put my own momma in the ground, would I even be able to find her?*

And somewhere in the center of the heat, the Spark ignited.

I don't remember who saw it first. We had been working on individual rubbings, our backs toward one another, when it seemed that some unseen lightning force jolted us around at once. And there it was. Scrawled in orange crayon above the gilded PRESTON, was MABLE, in big block letters.

"Who did that?" I whispered, afraid that I might awaken something. There was no answer.

We all stared at one another. No one was especially close to the scene of the crime, and the weapon of choice had been dropped at the foot of the headstone. Meg could not be ruled out, because even though she was little, she copied letters for Momma all the time.

And though I had no memory of the act, I could not even exclude myself from blame. I'd heard that people who got hit by lightning usually didn't remember it afterward.

"Giiiiiiiiiirls! Come on! Let's go!" Momma yelled. And with that, we left the "invisible hand" incident right where it happened. We never told Momma and Kit, or spoke of it to one another.

That night, for the last time I can remember, Momma and Kit got a quiet car ride home from Damascus. They thought we were all just too worn out to talk. I think we were all just listening to the hum we had created among us, and watching the cloud of fireflies that seemed to light up and dance to it around the PRESTON grave, and followed us all the way home.

I recorded that miracle later, as a parable in my Bible notebook, so that it might account for future happenings in my Christian life that an ignorant soul might interpret as sinful-on-purpose. The Spark accounted for a lot in the spiritual goings-on of people, I thought, and children in particular. It gave us power we could not have alone, and protected us from blame we should not share alone. Any good Southern church-goer would attest that some kind of collective electricity could be felt in the congregation on Sunday mornings. This only made sense. For reasons I've yet to figure out, though, it was not exactly the cousin-style Spark of exhilarating joy. It was a different kind of current, and sometimes it even made me feel bad. Or guilty. Or afraid. Or nothing.

AFFLICTED

After the incident with Mr. Nick and the holiest-garment contest, Daddy spent a lot of time reminding me that Baptists believe all saved souls are equal. No one is any holier than the person next to her in the eyes of Jesus; we are all sinners and we are all saints and we are all ornery and awful and perfect at once, and everything is even and level as a hundred-year-old pew.

Of course, this seemed a little unfair to me. Not only that, but I was sure there was an insult to Jesus's common sense in there somewhere. I did not seriously think that the son of God was so holy-blind that He was like the kids in my class who got sent away once a week on a van with Miss Schott because they were in the "special club" of people who could not tell the difference between a school chair and a toilet.

Still, I would nod out of respect for my elder every time Daddy told me that part-truth, because I knew it was what he had to say. All Christian parents had to speak in part-truths when it came to discussing important things with their children, because another key part of the Baptist doctrine is that a child cannot withstand pure truth until he is at least seventeen or eighteen. Before that his soul is too delicate, and any knowledge that you don't water down a bit will burn it out. Or at the very least, it will burn the ends of his fingertips and tinge the white parts of his eyes red, as if he's opened them in a pool with too much chlorine. (These were the symptoms I had seen inflicted on certain teenagers from our congregation, who came dragged-by-the-shirttail to our front door in the middle of the night by sobbing mommas who carried little white, cigarette-shaped objects in plastic bags. The explanation Daddy gave me for those children's symptoms, shaking his head and sighing, was always the same: "It seems they just learned a few things too early. Very, very dangerous to learn some things too early." I knew better than to beg for any more details from him, so I just took his words under advisement. The next time I snuck into Daddy's study to open the thickest church book he owned, the one with the slick pages and the paintings of the prophets and the teeniest print, I wore a pair of my momma's yellow dish gloves to protect my hands from the knowledge.)

Later on, I just assumed that Daddy's talk of equality was his way of putting a dish glove over my eternal virtue. Any less learned child might have just called it an outright lie, though, because anyone who has spent much time in a Southern Baptist Church can tell you that this isn't really how it works at all. In fact, I could think of several ways in which a Baptist could elevate herself to an untouchable level of holiness.

The best way you could become a Baptist soul of the highest order was to die, and to do it as a young person. If you could manage it, this dying needed to be done in some long and drawn-out way (though a car accident would work, too, in a pinch), and it needed to have someone to pin the blame on. I don't mean that you had to have been murdered to achieve Baptist sainthood, oh not at all! I just mean that your death had to be the sort that was useful in one of Mrs. Mounts's Sunday School lessons about how sinful the world could be.

For example, the first child I knew of to be crowned with righteousness in this way was Betty Claremore, a pale little bit of a thing who joined our church with her family after her bones were already half eaten with some terrible cancer. (I'd think, all the times I prayed for poor Betty, of how unfortunate it was that Betty's family hadn't been directed to a house of God just a few months earlier, because then she might have stood a chance.) The Sunday morning after Betty's funeral, Mrs. Mounts, sniveling into a Kleenex tissue so used and reused that it was practically crumbling with grief, had told us that it was a shame today's doctors were so preoccupied with some *other* disease—one that certain men had brought on *themselves*, she said—that they no longer had the time to come up with cures for poor souls like Betty. Then we all bowed and praised Betty's name.

For the next month, we all ran races in Betty's honor, past utility poles plastered with Betty's pictures. We gave prayers about her and even to her, and planted rosebushes in the church playground with plaques that bore her face. Some of our parents, who had let us send out our own homemade Christmas cards in the past, replaced them with cards that had a photocopied sketch of a star on the front, drawn by Betty in her last days. Betty Claremore was not only the first child I ever knew who died, but also the first true awe-inspiring celebrity I could ever say I knew personally.

It wasn't until months after the funeral, when we were taking up an offering for a benevolence fund for Betty's family, that I noticed a new face at the organ. Sometime during all the festivities surrounding Betty's young and joyous ascent to heaven, Mattie Reed, church pianist since before I was born— who had never hesitated to let me sit down beside her and touch the keys—had quietly passed away.

I had not even noticed.

I had not even stirred during the hour of my nap time that it had taken Daddy to perform Mattie's funeral. Racked with guilt, I sat on her piano seat and prayed a fast prayer for her soul one day while the sanctuary cleared out.

I did not dwell long on Mattie's passing, though. I realized our church had simply figured out that Mattie Reed had been a Christian so long, she could find her own way to heaven just fine. She didn't need the light of a thousand candlelight vigils to guide her, or the comfort of hymn choruses from mourning crowds that filled stadiums, the way Betty had. No, at the end of a long life in the Southern Baptist Church, Mattie Reed had been given peace and quiet as her just reward. I supposed that was fair.

But I thought I was destined for just a bit more in the holy hierarchy and history of King's Way Baptist Church. And I decided that the time of my promotion into the second-grade Sunday School class was the time to start my ascension. God had shown me through Betty that even a child of my age could achieve greatness of a biblical degree—her poor struggle could inspire newspaper stories about church fund drives that spread Jesus's goodness far and wide; prayer offerings for her could put painted murals of the Garden of Eden on hospital walls. Yes, God had a lot to thank Betty for, and I did not eat a single meal the summer she passed away without first being thankful for her sacrifice, and second being a little envious that it wasn't me who inspired such holy passion in God's people.

Of course, I knew that God did not intend for *me* to die. He wanted me to be a force that would draw people together, just as Betty had, but for a longer period of time than she had managed, perhaps due to her beginner praying skills. (Also, though I kept this revelation between myself and the Father, I think He knew the Christmas cards I drew would make the missions fund a lot more money in the long run, seeing as how the stars I drew weren't lopsided. Not that I believed they were better than Betty's; I just supposed that the skill needed to draw them was a gift He passed to me and me alone. I accepted it with humility.)

So the way I saw it, I only had one option to fulfill my holy destiny. I'd take advantage of the special truth God had revealed to me through Betty's dying—that while passing out tracts with a magician's flourish and knitting sweaters for the cold were great missionary-talents of Baptists, their most inspired endeavors came when someone, *anyone*, got sick as a dog. For nearly a year, I had been witness to the great Southern Baptist artistry of working in human suffering the way that some people could carve in marble or compose in music. Withered old church ladies who spent most of their time moaning and drooping off the front pews had suddenly become invigorated when the word came down that a soul was on its way out. Suddenly enough fruitcakes got baked to rebuild Jericho. Suddenly the church recreation committee finally had the money to rebuild the softball field (and if the wasting child who inspired it lasted long enough, she might even be able to see it for herself). Suddenly there were no complaints. Just joy out of sorrow like wine from water.

I decided that the only way a kid my age could hope to really make the church take notice, could even dream of inspiring enough of God's glory to get her own name in the front of an honorary pew hymnal, would be to toe the line between distressed and divine for a while herself. I decided I'd volunteer to become afflicted—sick, but holy. And famous. But with a purpose, of course.

When God was finished working through me, I reasoned, I would just pray myself back to health. That part I was sure about. Sure, from time to time, and especially when we made our Sunday visits to Mimi's bedside, doubt stuck its little forked tail into my heart. *What if you try this and you can only pray yourself partway out? What if you get stuck, like Mimi? Even Daddy can't help you then. You've seen in his eyes that he doesn't even know how. If he did, why wouldn't she be well—*

I pushed the thoughts from my mind, as hard and fast as I could, and told myself that this was the kind of internal abuse all good martyrs had to deal with. I focused, instead, on how to get God to hand me the affliction. I did not dare ask my parents or my grandparents, and especially not Memaw. Every time she shoved Meg and me up against some nursing home bedrail and made us sing Christmas carols, she always whispered in our ears, "You'd better thank the Lord for your own health, girls! And for the fact that you can sing so joyfully today, while others cannot." Her minty breath mixing over the bedpan smell was always just about enough to make me lose my health all over the floor then and there, but I could not sass her. Besides, I knew Memaw would never understand that I was not asking God to make me diseased; I was simply offering myself as a vehicle for his next wonder-working plague. Someone, somewhere was going to be chosen for affliction next. I might as well offer myself up, because I knew my temple could handle it.

Since I could not go to my family for help with this mission, I decided I would seek the assistance of our Catholic neighbor, Mary Anna. Now, this took a bit of noble courage on my part, because Mary Anna Stinson was so strange to me that I was almost frightened of her. She was my age but went to another school, one that required her to dress up almost every single day. On the rare chance that Meg and I ever saw Mary Anna outside while we played with her brothers (who were oddly dirty-faced and normal), she floated past our neighborhood mud pits like a ghost, elevated on her sacred petticoats.

The first time I'd gotten up the nerve to speak to her had been the Saturday of the last Easter weekend, when Meg and I were in the backyard, running through the sprinkler. Mary Anna had drifted out of the house in a little veil and long white dress that looked like a bridal gown. Her mother snapped pictures from the doorway but didn't step out any farther. I asked Momma if I could yell at Mary Anna and ask her if we might play dress-up too, but Momma just shook her head and held a finger to her mouth.

For a moment, I put my hands on my hips and started to protest Momma's shushing. I could see the sun bouncing off the tiny pearled rims of Mary Anna's puffed sleeves, and I could picture my own suntanned arms slipping delicately through them, wasted as they were on poor Mary Anna's paper-white frame. But another look from Momma put that idea right out of my head. (I didn't care what Mrs. Mounts said about psychic powers being instruments of Satan worshippers only. My momma had always been able to hold a mouth shut with nothing but a glance. Moses's parting of the Red Sea didn't take half the strength my momma's sharp brown eyes used on Meg's mouth every time we sat behind Mrs. Beets and her lopsided wig in Sunday service.)

Instead it was Momma herself who went over and spoke to Mary Anna, after taking some time to knot a towel over her own bathing suit (which I thought was odd, considering Momma wasn't wet and hadn't even set foot in the Snoopy sprinkler).

"We're planning to grill some hot dogs later, if you and your mother want to come on over," Momma offered. Mary Anna took a step backward out of Momma's shadow, as if it might stain her dress.

"Well, thank you," Mary Anna cooed, folding her hands in front of her. "But my mother doesn't have time to . . . to . . ."

From where I was standing, I could see Mary Anna's eyes pointing upward, searching the insides of her forehead the way I always did when I couldn't recall a Bible memory verse.

". . . she doesn't have *time* to . . . *bask* in the sun."

And with that, Mary Anna Stinson gave some sort of strange little bow to my mother and ran back into the house. Part of me hoped she'd fall and get grass stains down the front of her dress, but of course she didn't. Staring back at us from the Stinson's sliding-glass door like the Queen of Sheba (after she had her skin and soul bleached), Mary Anna's skirts and tights were white and her hair was almost white and even her patent-leather shoes were without so much as a scuff.

"It must be nice to have a heart so pure that your feet don't even touch the ground," my momma murmured, casting off her towel into a lawn chair while Mrs. Stinson lowered the blinds over the door. I asked Momma what she meant; wasn't it a *good* thing to be pure of heart?

Momma just laughed and fanned herself with her *Redbook* magazine, which a few moments before had been stuffed inside a copy of *HomeLife*, the magazine for Christian mothers.

I glanced back at the Stinsons' house, where I thought I saw the blinds flutter and shut again. I hoped Mrs. Stinson could see how beautiful my mother was, laughing and near naked in the sun like that. In fact, I wished all of our neighborhood could come in our backyard and see my momma, Sharon Hancock, prettiest woman in any town. I knew she could never be like Jessie Seger's mother, who chaperoned our class trip to the zoo in her big new perm and red high heels and Jordaches no wider than a pop can. (Mrs. Seger had nearly caused a riot among the second-grade boys in the draw for chaperone assignments.) No, my momma had to keep a buried beauty, under layers of choir robes and shoulder pads and sharp, foreboding steeples. The subject of what God had given her would forever be a secret, embarrassing thing, except to those of us with access to our little backyard. In that little corner of grass, among her geraniums, her girls, and her laughter, was the pastor's wife's secret temple. Mrs. Stinson wouldn't have been worthy enough to worship there if she wrapped herself in a hundred yards of the finest pearl-edged pinafores.

". . . I just think," Momma replied, "and please don't repeat this in front of church people or your dad, but I think the best hearts have just a *little* sin; just to give the Good Lord something to work with. Just enough to weigh you down so your feet can touch the ground, like regular folks. Just a *little* bit of weight is all it takes . . ."

Momma had many more important spiritual thoughts to give her eldest, I was sure, but her speech was interrupted by Meg, who was screaming and laughing like a banshee across the lawn. Her training pants had gotten waterlogged and fallen off on the head of the Snoopy sprinkler. Just a little bit of weight was all it took, and I had to admit it did make Christian life interesting.

Still, more than a year after that backyard incident, when I went to Mary Anna's door to seek her help with my affliction project, I made sure to first wash every bit of sinful "weight" off me, twice—every bit of dirt, every ounce of hidden meanness I could think of. It was a baptism with Momma's big bar of green soap, the kind that she said would be too harsh on my skin and Meg's, swiped from her shower without permission only because it was an emergency (and any Christian will tell you that all sins are off in an emergency).

I couldn't be sure why my hands were so driven to do all that scrubbing, but it was almost as if I feared the Stinsons would have a hidden sin detector on their front porch. Maybe something like the "Jehovah's Witness Ejection System" I'd heard my grandfather talk about installing.

One Friday afternoon, when I'd decided my mission could wait no longer, I waited until Momma was elbow-deep in dishwater and the weekly phone call from Aunt Kit. Then I tiptoed out of the house and across to the Stinsons' front yard.

I got up to their front door and tapped so lightly at first that I could be sure they didn't hear it. My nerves teased heat off my body, and the scent of Momma's soap filled the porch. I realized that I was standing on my tiptoes for no good reason.

The soap, I mumbled to myself, *now* that *was a mistake.*

Because now I smelled like a woman. Memaw had pointed out to me time and time again the woe that came to girls who tried to look, act, or smell anything other than their age.

I decided I'd go home and wash again, then come back. But it was too late.

"Can I help you?"

Mary Anna was peering around the front door like some fluffy little dungeon-keeper.

"No, I was just . . ." I went up and down on my toes, and I steeled myself. *The Lord's work takes courage, Emy. You know that. If it was something you enjoyed, then it wouldn't be the Lord's work, now, would it?*

". . . I mean . . . yes. I need to know how you pray for . . . well, just tell me how you pray for something really big. Something that might have to do with a sickness and that only God would understand."

I said the words as quickly as possible and closed my eyes right afterward. The confused, tilted glance would come, I was certain; the curious, the reverent *But your daddy is the preacher!*

Had I been in Mary Anna's position, the question would have knocked my understanding of the world's spiritual hierarchy right off its bearings. How could *I*, the daughter of the Reverend Hancock, have any possible need of any holy advice from *her*? She who'd worn a full-fledged bridal getup in the front yard, when my grandmother Mimi herself had once warned me, "A young girl turning up in a wedding gown all of a sudden means only one thing, and you're too young to know, but there isn't a thing holy about it."

The truth was, though it broke my heart to admit any

weakness of Daddy's, it was he who'd always said that no one respected being tortured in the name of the Lord like the Catholics. From the little I understood of it, if Mary Anna ever hoped to reach the highest level of her own church, she wasn't just going to have to become afflicted, she was going to have to be set on fire.

"Here."

Mary Anna's reply, which came much sooner than I had expected and had not an ounce of confusion around its edges, jarred my eyes open. She was holding out a little square leather book. It was almost as thick as it was wide.

"My mother uses this when she prays for weighty matters, and things always happen. It's in Latin and it's called a *missal*," Mary Anna said. She pushed that last word out of her mouth slowly and made the movements of her lips really wide and obvious, as if I were deaf and would need to lip-read. She thrust the book toward me, catching the door frame to balance herself. Mary Anna looked deathly afraid of letting her pure white lacy socks touch the worldly territory beyond the threshold.

I almost reached for the book, but then I caught her eyes. I caught her eyes and her eyes caught onto the floor of my stomach.

I knew that look—head cocked a little to one side, chin down, forehead wrinkled far too much for a little girl. This was not a look of confused reverence, or of crazy-neighbor curiosity. No, this was a look I knew too well. Underneath the weight of a sigh, with what I could swear was a *tsk-tsk* hidden somewhere at the back of it, Mary Anna Stinson was giving me the Missionary Gaze.

Now, I can describe the Gaze best by saying that you can't describe it in terms of what it looks like. You just know it when you feel it hit you in the guts. By the time I came face-to-face with it on the Stinsons' porch, I had seen people like Mrs. Mounts master the Gaze through years of devoted Christian stewardship. Even Miss Geneva, with her airy, blinking, friendly-as-the-daylight eyelashes, had bestowed it from time to time, usually when a poor child came to Sunday School without so much as a necktie or sweater-vest. Yes, I knew that look. It said, *I always knew it would come to this. I always knew someone like* you *would need to come to* me *for help. I've just been here, waiting.*

The problem was, I had thought up until that moment with Mary Anna that it was only Baptists who could give the Gaze so skillfully. Part of our devoted missions training was learning to baptize someone with pity using our eyes alone; to make them feel—*feel*—deep down, that Christian charity was not free at all. Just as Christ paid for the world's sins with His blood, the needy had to know what it was like to pay for holy goodness. They could pay by giving up a little of their pride. The Gaze was the best way of drawing that payment out of them, slowly and sweetly. They'd appreciate it one day, Lord willing.

I staggered backward from the Stinsons' doorway, trying with all my strength not to look up into that face again. Somewhere, beyond Mary Anna Stinson's downy eyebrows, there was a prayer for my soul going on. I could almost hear it. Like a funeral march for all my Baptist dignity, I could hear it.

"Don't you want to look at it?" Mary Anna went on. I shook my head, keeping it low. Down at the bottom of the doorway, I could see the small space between the hem of her dress and the tops of her socks, where her legs were an ethereal shade of porcelain for July. I was suddenly so aware of my own summer legs, which Momma had once said could be sold to the Museum of Modern Art. They were a canvas of little blond fuzz, skinned scab patches, peeling tan, and calamine.

I crossed my worse marked leg behind the other and stood there balancing, like a fool bird that had to pee real bad. Out of the corner of my eye, I could tell Mary Anna was still holding out that missile, or whatever she had called it, her Gaze locked and loaded.

Suddenly—and I don't know whether it was the humidity or the fool-bird pose that kept blood from getting up to my brain—I started to feel dizzy. Wisps of bleach and vinegar seeped from the Stinsons' front hallway and circled about my head, and I could feel my heart beating faster in the heat.

"N . . . no," I managed, finally. "I have to go home. Thank you for showing me the book but I . . . I do not have time to . . . to *bask*."

I turned around and jumped off the front porch so quickly that I hoped Mary Anna wouldn't be able to read my face. She might figure out that I didn't really understand what that *bask* word meant. I knew only how quickly it had ended my mother's own attempted Missionary Gaze effort with Mary Anna, so I thought I would use it again.

I ran back through the grass toward home, listening for Mary Anna to call me back in protest, but she never did. In my soul, I knew she wouldn't. She didn't need to. She'd made me feel the uncomfortable fuzzy warmth of the Gaze without my even looking at her.

One day, I'd have to return the favor and lower Mary Anna a few notches with my own sweet looks when she came begging. That was the only way to balance the scales, to make us equal again in God's eyes. And that was what real missions work was all about, I decided. Balancing the scales.

Yes, one day I'd return the charity. It was the only right and righteous thing to do.

Lesson 5

Momma "basking"

Goodness

GOOD CHRISTIAN WOMEN

She is just a good, solid Christian woman. She really is."

This was always my momma's catchall description when she couldn't think of anything particularly outstanding to say about a woman.

"Yes, she is, she really is," Aunt Kit repeated, nodding at Dottie Jane and me in the rearview mirror between jolted swipes of lip gloss. She and Momma recited this same two-line dialogue at least fifty times during the trip to the oldest and most rotting part of Damascus, to the home of Aunt Sylvania Campbell. It was as if they thought saying it over and over would add more weight to it, would help to smooth the journey and flatten the jutting cobblestones that made Dottie Jane and me jump like popcorn every ten feet, and would make the whole trip seem like it had some logical sense to it.

I had never been to Aunt Vaney's house in my life. To tell you the truth, up until that day if someone had asked me where Aunt Vaney lived, I might have said, *Why, I believe she stays propped up in a long box next to the Christmas decorations.* Because to me, that's what Vaney Campbell was. A holiday fixture. The only time I ever saw her was when she was backlit by the fireplace once a year, slouched and stilled in one of Mimi's mahogany living room chairs, as if she'd been carved a part of it.

Technically, we all knew, she was some kind of a relative—
one of Grandma Mimi's cousins, if Momma's memory served
correctly (and Mimi herself had been asleep and unable to
confirm it for some time). But it seemed that somewhere
along the way, as a reward for her time served with the family,
and for looking solid and Christian, she'd been upgraded to an
aunt. So that was what everyone called her.

But as we pulled into the gravel dent-in-the-grass that was
Aunt Vaney's driveway, I was reminded that in the Bluegrass, a
familiar title didn't mean diddly-squat in terms of your real-
life comfort with a person. Several of my classmates went by
"Little Randy" or "Little Bill," as if the *Little* was a title bestowed out of great devotion (even though we all knew it was
really the fading footprint of a "Big Randy" or "Big Bill," who
hadn't seen his child in years). And of course, there was always
a new "Buddy" darkening the playground year after year, who
always proved to be the orneriest child you could ever hope
to meet.

No, I just could not wait for whatever was in store for me
in an afternoon with this "aunt."

It didn't surprise me that Dottie Jane wasn't so fearful.

"Momma, can I borrow your hairbrush? I look a mess,"
she said, straightening the fasteners of her red OshKosh
jumper as if they were bra straps. On a reflex, I made a show
of scooting over and checking my own bangs in the side mirror, even though the whole concept of "looking a mess" had
not occurred to me until just then. Though she was a year
younger than me and almost a full head shorter, being in the
presence of Dottie Jane Bennington always made me feel like
some dowdy, unsophisticated ruffian-child. She never left the

house without nail polish (in a bright red color that Momma wouldn't let me try out in public) that matched her socks that matched her hair ribbon, and that evening she was getting something called a "home permanent" as part of her birthday present.

Of course, being the child prodigy of one of the top theologians in all of the state, I hardly considered myself unworldly. But next to my little cousin, who seemed to have been raised by a mystic cult of seventeen-year-old cheerleaders, I could not help but be a little in awe.

"Don't worry," Dottie Jane reassured, patting me on the shoulder in a way I'd only seen grown-up women do to other grown-up women. "Suzanne's old outfit looks really great on you. Really, it does, the fit is perfect."

I knew that this was Dottie Jane's sincerest form of a compliment, and to tell you the truth, I didn't care if it wasn't. I'd been eyeing the skirt and T-shirt, which had bears drawn in puffed paint ringing the hems and collar, ever since Suzanne had worn it to our family reunion the year before. I knew I only had to be patient until the time when Aunt Kit made her twice-yearly "cleaning-out" visit, the back of her station wagon full to the top with clothes that she, Suzanne, and Dottie Jane had bought in the previous six months and would never wear again.

But Dottie's words seemed to have hit Momma differently. No one else in the car even noticed it, but I saw her pause for a second when Dottie gave me the compliment. She started picking at the side of her thumbnail, and this was always a dead giveaway that my mother was worried about something. The preacher's wife kept her burdens buried deeply in her nail beds.

I decided to make a joke, to make Momma stop the nail picking.

"Yes, it does look good," I proclaimed to the car. "It is a good, solid, Christian outfit, with even better, solid-er Christian dancing bears."

Well, everyone just cracked up at this, including (thank you, Lord) Momma, who put down her thumb and addressed the backseat.

"Ha ha ha . . . but now, you all remember, like we said, no laughing and no making fun once we get out of this car. You two be good. Aunt Vaney is doing us a favor by keeping you."

"Why can't we just go with *you* . . ." Dottie Jane whined. She'd begun to fan herself quickly with one hand, even though it wasn't hot in the car.

"You heard what Aunt Sharon said, Dottie Jane," Aunt Kit piped in. "All the adults have to go out and meet with Mimi's lawyers, so there's no one around right now to keep you . . ."

I was half surprised Aunt Kit didn't give a reverent pause when she spoke the word *lawyers*. None of us cousins were precisely clear on what these lawyers did; we knew only that our mothers (and even Daddy, to some extent) seemed to be placing more faith in them lately than they did in the Lord Almighty. At first, the church had rallied around my family with such fervor that I was shocked all their prayers, benefit suppers, and offerings failed to wake my grandmother for eternity. But after the first year, the fervor faded. After that, the only thing that seemed to really lift my mother's spirits was talk of these lawyers, and what mystical powers they might hold to heal our souls and make things right again.

". . . Now, you could have gone out to the pool with Meg and Clayton, but *some* people were concerned about what the chlorine would do to their precious little hair shafts."

Aunt Kit sucked in her cheeks and brushed her bangs aside with a flourish. I couldn't help laughing out loud at this, though one look from Dottie Jane let me know that my reaction was decidedly immature.

"I was afraid that it would make it so the . . . the *excelsia* in the home permanent wouldn't work!" she cried.

Now, I was quite sure that *excelsia* was not a real word. But that was hardly worth pointing out when Dottie Jane had one of these little fits. She'd always had the habit, when she got mad, of running together a few of the long words she'd heard adults around her say, then forming them into little, personalized, frustration-and-Coca-Cola-fueled fireballs that shot from her mouth before you knew what hit you. Then, after you thought about it, you realized you didn't have a single solitary clue what word it *was* that was supposed to have hit you. But you sure respected the holy heck out of it.

Maybe this was what gave Dottie Jane so much clout among our group of cousins, I thought. She was the tiniest, for sure, but she seemed to float so high above us all on her cloud of hair-sprayed glory that we couldn't ever hope to catch her reasoning, much less her language. So we didn't try.

The clang of Aunt Vaney's doorbell bounced around inside for a month or so before we finally heard footsteps, moving toward us from somewhere near the back.

"You sure she'll be okay watching little kids?" Aunt Kit whispered through gritted, smiling teeth.

"Oh, yes, Kit, don't be silly," Momma replied. "She's apparently one of the best volunteers they have down at the Special Souls mission. Lots of little children there, you know."

Momma forced a smile and nodded at me, as if it was me she needed to reassure, not my aunt. Or maybe the smile was another Momma plea, something like *Please, Emy, don't announce that the children at Special Souls wouldn't know a good volunteer from a bucketful of dishrags, because they're blind as bats.* But this was true.

Meanwhile, I could see Kit trying to drum up a reassurance impressive enough for Dottie Jane, who was picking slivers of peeling paint from a railing and wearing such a repulsed expression that you'd have thought the entire house had psoriasis. The best she could come up with was: "You know, Dottie Jane, Aunt Vaney was a regular beauty queen in her day. She had the most lovely, *lovely* features. I bet, back in her time, you'd just about never seen anyone so beautiful. Back in her time."

Dottie Jane did not acknowledge the pretty commentary. Instead she mumbled, "These are fake," and poked at a couple of misshapen wood shingles someone had put down to replace the broken porch tiles. You could tell that the tile had once been laid out in a beautiful blue-and-yellow sunburst pattern. Back in its time. Maybe there was potential for a good afternoon here, I started to wonder. One filled with discoveries of dust-covered beauty, and plenty of mysteries hidden in the corners of this cavernous house.

But when Aunt Vaney finally did open that front door, the mystery faded a bit. Nothing seemed "hidden" about that woman at all. In fact, everything about her was so big and up-my-nose (including a smell that was somewhere between talcum powder and Grandy's arthritis cream) that I couldn't imagine her being able to hide from anyone. Even standing up in the doorway (which she did not come down from to greet my mother and aunt, though this would have been polite), I could tell that she was at least half a foot taller than each of them, not counting the beehive hairdo that was threatening to destroy a spiderweb in the top left corner of the door frame.

Aunt Vaney didn't seem quite put together like a regular woman, either. Maybe she had been once—*beautifully*, as my mother had said—but it seemed that at some point Aunt Vaney's doctor, and the handyman she got to repair her porch, had become one and the same person. Where once there might have been beauty, Vaney's body now looked as if it had been put together and patched with cheaper, mismatched parts, the whole package refinished with coat after coat of peeling paint.

The odd angle of a collarbone jutted out from beneath a threadbare cardigan toward my throat as she leaned down toward my cousin and me.

"Well. Hello there, little girls." she said, not smiling. She looked more like she expected a curtsy or something. I knew that she didn't have any children of her own, so I told myself that she couldn't be expected to know that "hello, little girls" was a greeting used only by the Big Bad Wolf and the villains in molester-awareness filmstrips.

I couldn't resist looking over at Dottie Jane to see her reaction to our babysitter. I wondered if she was thinking about how much less flattering broad daylight was, compared with the glow of Mimi's Christmas tree.

But when my precious cousin finally opened her mouth, her words were of pure, Christian concern.

"Aunt Vaney," she pleaded, her little blond brows tightly knit. "May I *please* brush your hair?"

"Dottie Jane!" Aunt Kit snapped, gripping my cousin's shoulder. Kit's own shoulders seemed to hunker down a bit, the way mine did whenever I got corrected by my grandmother. "Vaney, she just . . . just loves to play beauty parlor! You know, how little girls do."

It sounded for a minute like Vaney might laugh, but it turned out she was just clearing her big, hanging, gobbler throat. Momma leaned down and whispered that Dottie Jane and I might want to run on inside while she took care of some last-minute sitter business. We slinked through the talcum-and-medicine barrier and made our way into what Vaney called "the parlor."

Now, I am certainly not being disrespectful to an elder when I say that the inside of Aunt Vaney's house reminded me of the inside of Lazarus's tomb. It wasn't that it was dirty, oh not at all. It looked and smelled clean as can be. But it seemed clean in a dirty kind of way— things weren't shining because they were cared for; they were shining because no one had touched them in a hundred years or so. Over the sofa, where an old painting of a farm landscape hung slightly off kilter, I could see where the wallpaper had completely faded around it, and a faint ring of soot marked the frame's proper place. An old lockbox, hand-labeled GREEN STAMPS in script so delicate that I just knew the writer was one of those old-timey Victorian ladies who had to use a quill, sat on a sideboard near the door. I thought it probably had a faded rim around it, too, if you moved it. But no dust, anywhere. No, it was as though some long-dead ghost had taken up residence in the rambling old place, whisking sheets off all the furniture just before company came over. (I shuddered at this last thought, remembering what my teenage cousin Carl had whispered in my ear last year at Christmas—that Aunt Vaney had died two Thanksgivings ago, but they fixed her so that you could wind her up and get her moving again. She always had a perfect curlicue at the back of her beehive, and this was where they put in the crank to wind her.)

Strangest of all, though, was the room's main decoration. On a shelf that went all the way around the parlor walls, Aunt Vaney seemed to have every Christmas card she'd ever gotten in her entire life on display. They were lined up in groups of size and color, with the fanciest ones directly across from the front door, right where arriving company could see them. Most were faded out from the sunlight of June-after-June in a row, but a few still held their sparkle. And these, of course, held Dottie Jane's attention from the start.

"Oh. It's not real velvet," she whispered, sniffing the cover of an especially heavy, especially well-gilded card. I wanted badly to look inside, because I was sure Mrs. Mounts had probably sent it, though I couldn't say how she knew Aunt Vaney. Mrs. Mounts always cleaned out the Hallmark of the fanciest cards before anyone else could get to them, or so I'd heard Mrs. Hamilton say outside the choir room. The practice was prideful and mocked the infant Jesus, she'd said.

"Now, now, little girls!" came Aunt Vaney's sudden croak. "You are not to touch those! Those do not belong to you, little girls."

"My *name* is *Dottie Jane Benn-ing-ton*," Dottie spouted.

I held my breath and tried not to show my joy at her sass.

One thing was for sure—you could go anywhere, even into the darkest, dullest, most long-abandoned tomb in the depths of the earth, and you would not have a boring afternoon as long as my cousin Dottie Jane was with you. She could conjure orneriness out of old socks. More than that, she proved the point that I was planning to write into my Bible notebook as soon as possible: that a little misbehaving is not bad at the hands of one cousin (or bretheren, that word sounded better). For it keepeth the rest of the flock entertained long enough so that they might not stir up a bigger mischief. And blessed is she who sacrifices her own good behavior for the sake of others.

But this time, Dottie's sacrifice was in vain. Aunt Vaney didn't even scold her with her eyes. She just moved her mouth back and forth a bit, as if she might think about making a remark, then smoothed out all the pile on the velvet card and placed it back on the shelf without a word.

Aunt Vaney spent the next few minutes rearranging the cards around it and making little measurements with her fingers and thumb. She even took off her glasses at one point and got her head way down close to the cards, like a strange kid inspecting an ant farm. Dottie Jane and I just moved backward and sat on the couch to stare at her. What else was a child supposed to do?

Finally, she turned toward us and started to speak. But then she seemed to think better of it, and she moved to the other side of the coffee table and talked to us from back there, like she was teaching a class on the first day of school or something.

"There now," she said, leaning over like a lightning-struck oak. I could smell her breath from the couch, and though I loved Dottie Jane's mischief, I was secretly praying that she would not notice the smell. "If you'll please not to touch any-thing else, I think we'll have a very nice afternoon."

Dottie Jane raised her hand. I felt my neck straighten up.

"Aunt Vaney, can we watch the TV?"

It was only then that I noticed what Dottie Jane had sniffed out right away—what I had thought might be some kind of old-fashioned washing machine was, in fact, a television. It was made up of a wooden box almost as big as my whole bed at home, but the screen part of it was little and round, like a sau-cer. Like a giant grasshopper-turned-human might have flown to earth in it and set up housekeeping.

At this request, Aunt Vaney's mouth commenced to work-ing back and forth faster than ever. Finally, she said, "Well, I did not ask your mothers whether or not television was appropri-ate or allowed. So no."

Dottie Jane made an audible deflating sound next to me. After learning what the mysterious washing machine really was, I wanted to sigh, too. But instead, I mustered my courage and asked, "Then what should we play with, ma'am?"

Here now, I reassured Dottie Jane with a wink, *this will be good.* Despite the Martian-like feeling I always got upon en-tering all the old people's houses I'd visited in my life, I'd man-aged to have the most surprisingly fun visits there. As Memaw had taught me early on, old people liked to have young people come and play. It was a blessing from the Lord to them, in an afternoon otherwise filled with nothing but day-old sugar-free candy and fuzzy Robert Schuller broadcasts. Seldom had I left an elder's home without a handful of old perfume bottles or costume jewelry, or a lesson in how you do magic tricks with a quarter, or how the Japanese could not be trusted.

Aunt Vaney's eyes swept the room, pausing for a dangerously long time on a yellowed paperback on the coffee table
called *Learn to Play Bridge in a Day.*

But she didn't pick up the book. She didn't pick up anything. She just reminded us, again, that we were good Christian
little girls, and surely we could be trusted to sit quietly—on
the couch *only*—and entertain ourselves. She would be at her
desk in the other room, preparing her Bible study lesson.

"Well for heaven's sake," Dottie Jane whispered when our
babysitter was finally out of earshot. The curlicue in the back
of Aunt Vaney's beehive still peered ominously at us from the
far end of the other room. Turning on the TV low, or playing house with the collection of little ceramic doggies on the
plant stand, without getting caught, didn't seem to be a likely
prospect.

Dottie Jane and I just stared at each other. I think both of
us felt a little afraid to move from the edge of the couch. We'd
never been left in a situation like this before—ordered not
to move under the threat of the apocalypse—unless we were
being severely punished or in church. But Dottie Jane was not
a regular church attendee. She had no comment on our situation, except to say, "Being a good Christian is as boring as the
daylights. Are you sure your Jesus didn't die of being *bored?*"

Somewhere, from a far corner of the upstairs, the faint
voice of Hank Williams singing gospel wafted down the stairs.
I wondered whether Hank himself was tied up somewhere up
there, in a trunk or under the bed or something. *This seems like
the kind of house where he might be,* I thought. Then I pushed the
evil thought out of my mind and asked the Lord for forgiveness, because I could not imagine how I'd let it creep into my

head. My cousin might not have been theologically learned, but she was right about one thing: It was far too easy to sin when you had to just sit there and think for yourself. I thought of Mrs. Mounts, and all the church's most sanctified Women's Missionary Union ladies, many of whom didn't work and had nothing to do but sit in their sanctified houses all day long. How they managed to keep their minds so holy and pure through all that was beyond me.

Marooned on the couch, even Dottie Jane seemed to have been abandoned by the mischief that usually followed her around at all times. She wriggled back onto the seat, and finally seemed defeated by the sagging weight of the house, and the sad sag of Aunt Vaney, and the sag of sunlight through the cloudy window that seemed to be stretching the day as long as possible.

But then Aunt Vaney's couch cushions broke their silence. Forever baptized in its individual, clear-plastic cover, Dottie Jane's cushion made a loud *Pffffffffffffffffffffffffttttt!* as she wriggled into place.

Well this, of course, made my cousin crack up so loud that the laughter threatened to topple the delicate Christmas card display. I managed to keep from joining her, and to keep my good Christian dignity, for about half a second.

We were having such a good time that we didn't notice how Aunt Vaney's Bible study pencil had frozen, her elbow poised in midair. Slowly, the laser-curlicue began to move as she swung around toward us. Her face was red.

"Little girls!" Aunt Vaney shouted. "I have never! Please, let's try to show some manners when we are a guest in someone's home! Say excuse me!"

Dottie Jane and I were stunned by her sudden anger, and for a moment we did feel ashamed of ourselves. For what, we weren't sure. And then we realized what Aunt Vaney thought had happened. This time, I started the cracking up. Dottie Jane started laughing so hard that she could barely point and say "It was Emy! Emy did it!"

I had no defense. In truth, part of me wished I had done it. Being in Aunt Vaney's house was just like being in Sunday service, and that deep demon that always seemed to find me when everything was most quiet, most holy, and prod me to raise the roof somehow, was here.

Vaney looked paralyzed. She was mad, but she knew she was powerless. I wondered if that meant there was some memory of her own Spark buried deep within her, after all. Maybe it was in the corner of her brain that had been preserved with umpteen layers of Aqua Net. The back of her puffed head looked almost as if it were under a thin layer of glass.

Finally, she shook her head and turned back toward her Bible.

I breathed a sigh of relief. The moment out of boredom had been wonderful, but I knew I could never be as free of heart as Dottie Jane. Whether she had a good reason to be or not, Aunt Vaney, an adult, had gotten upset with me, and I wondered if she would tell my mother. Even if I'd just watched Aunt Vaney rob a bank, I'd have still felt guilty as the daylights if she threatened to "tell" on me. The fact that I hadn't actually done anything wrong didn't matter. In my world, wrongs became wrongs when they were declared from the mouths of elders.

Dottie Jane, of course, had a different thought. She'd gotten a taste of entertainment for the day, and now there would be no stopping her. Before I could hold her back, she had flitted across the room and was tapping Aunt Vaney's shoulder.

"Yes?" Vaney said, not turning around. Her voice almost quivered, as if the sight of a restless child would turn her into a pillar of salt. If she wasn't one already.

"Is that you in that picture?" Dottie Jane asked. "Are you the bride?"

I hadn't noticed the oval portrait hanging above Vaney's writing desk. And if I had, I certainly wouldn't have called it a "bride." All the brides I'd ever seen wore a long white uniform of a train and veil. They weren't standing outside a courthouse or wearing a suit. That seemed undignified to the Lord's blessed union. And it was much less pretty.

"Yes," Vaney answered. "Yes, that is me, and that was very long ago. Now if you'll please let me—"

"Why aren't you still married? Did he die?"

Suddenly the room was filled with nothing but Hank's murmurs. I should have known. I should have pulled Dottie Jane back the moment she got up. *How did I always seem to forget that what would start as a bit of fun with my cousins, a touch of wildness of the kind Meg and I rarely saw, always turned into something none of us could control by the end of the night?* It was like a storm center settled over whatever spot we got together, and a few playful sparks of lightning started the winds to snapping, and they popped and snapped and fed off one another until orneriness was its own tornado that none of us could stop. "Let's play some music" always led to "Let's be rock stars," which had once somehow lead to one of my father's dress shirts being cut up and streaked with Magic Markers and two of his record albums being smashed. My mother's brand-new mixer had been ruined the night Momma gave us all permission to try to make our own ice pops. My cousins could seldom leave well enough alone, and Meg and I didn't have the nerve to make them try.

Dottie Jane's innocent questioning had *Disaster* written all over it. Luckily, though, Aunt Vaney didn't seem to be getting sucked into the game.

"No. We are divorced. That is the end of that story."

"But can't you get married again?" Dottie Jane asked. I felt my bottom tense up so tight that I almost went sliding straight off the slippery cushions. Vaney put her pencil down and faced forward, talking to the wall. She still wasn't willing to dignify Dottie Jane's prodding with eye contact. For that, I had to admire her.

"I cannot get married again, because I am divorced. You may have your mother read you what the Bible says about that. I do not have time to explain it all to you today."

Dottie Jane didn't seem satiated, but she knew she wasn't going to get any further rise out of our babysitter. She wandered over to an armchair, where a stuffed, crocheted purple dog hung limply over the arm. Aunt Vaney's rear "eye" seemed to reactivate. She reminded Dottie Jane not to touch anything.

To my relief and disappointment, my cousin came back to the sofa. She picked up a Christmas card and started to fan herself with it, I think just for spite. This time, Aunt Vaney didn't notice.

"I know the reason she can't get married again," Dottie Jane whispered, holding the card sideways over our mouths, to make sure it was a real secret.

"Why?" I said. I had to admit, this was a part of the Bible with which I was not familiar. Even though I'd been through Sunday School since birth and knew every story there was to know, I seemed to be finding out about more and more of these "hidden truths" as I grew older. I did know that divorced men were not allowed to be deacons of the church. No one had ever told me where you could find this truth in the Bible, though it did make sense to me. Memaw had once said that divorced men had "forgotten how to be husbands." This probably meant that they couldn't be trusted to remember how you collect the offering plates, either.

"Because," Dottie Jane went on. She drew the card as close to her face as she could. "It's because her popo already bled."

"What?" I gasped. I would have giggled at the fact that Dottie Jane'd said *popo* out in public—one of our secret words—if I hadn't been so shocked.

"You don't know what you're talking about," I snapped. "You don't even read the Bible. There's nothing in there about a popo."

I instantly wished I could take back the part about Dottie Jane not reading the Bible. It was true, but I'd seen the hurt flash across her wide eyes when I said it. My cousin was not yet baptized, and I'd been told time and time again that I was called upon to be a witness for the unsaved. That meant it was probably all my fault that her biblical knowledge was so sparse. If she ever moved to east Kentucky, I knew she'd be beaten up every day at school for not knowing the difference between the epistles and the apostles. Yet here I was, spouting off like Miss Know-It-All. It was shameful. I decided to let her continue, without a fight.

"Yes it does! I swear! Jill Jeffries across the street told me, and they go to church fifty times a day or something. She said that when you get married, and you go to sleep that night, the girl's popo bleeds. And you can't get married ever again if the popo has bled, because the man can tell. And if you try, you get beat to death with rocks."

Dottie Jane's face was stone-solid. I shot a glance over my shoulder, unable to believe that the sheer force of what had just come out of my cousin's mouth had not roused Aunt Vaney from her chair. But she was hunched over, deep in prayer. And from what my cousin had just told me, she needed it.

I shook my head at Dottie Jane, as convincingly as I could. But this was hard. Dottie Jane had just quoted Jill Jeffries, a child I had met only a handful of times, but who might possibly have surpassed me in terms of biblical knowledge attained by age seven. I was not jealous of her, though. Every good Christian will tell you that Bible knowledge doesn't count unless you are driven to learn it by the Holy Spirit, not just because your momma makes you, and Jill Jeffries's mother was a master of making. Jill and her brother weren't even allowed to watch TV unless they first measured out ten feet from the screen with a tape measure, and sat behind that point on the carpet. And if they wanted to play outside they had to put on knee pads, even if we weren't riding bikes. Aunt Kit had once murmured that Kathy Jeffries felt the need to make the world padded all over, just for her kids. It was clear to me that the forced-learned scripture was just as good as thick cotton batting, in her eyes.

"I still don't believe you," I told Dottie Jane.

"It's true!" she shouted, shushing her mouth with her own

hand, a little too late. Aunt Vaney moved her head around part-way, but she didn't even bother scolding us this time. I hoped it was because the time when Momma and Kit would pick us up was getting closer.

"It's true," Dottie Jane whispered. "And you can even ask your dad. It's in the Book of Denver Enemy."

"There's no—"

"Yes there is. Yes there is, yes there is, *yes. There. Is.*" Dottie Jane's little brown eyes blazed with such conviction that I was shocked the Lord would waste it on a heathen. Then again, Memaw always said that the world's great supply of conviction was divided between Baptists and beauticians—they had that heaven-sent skill of putting a hand on the hip and saying "Now that is just the way it is" in such a way that no one in earshot needed further reassurance. Maybe Dottie Jane's great affection for home permanents was a sign that she had been blessed with the gift.

I didn't get to argue with her further, though. About a minute later, a soft "Amen" came from the other room, and Aunt Vaney appeared in the doorway.

"Well, I told your mothers I would send you home fed. What kind of sandwiches do y'all want?"

I prayed Dottie Jane wouldn't ask for a popo platter. She had done that before, at a restaurant that was not even Chinese. We had all started laughing because we couldn't help it, but the mommas spanked us later when they found out the waiter thought we were laughing at his lisp.

"I'll take grilled cheese, please," Dottie Jane said. I breathed a sigh of relief.

"Well, you may *have* peanut butter and jelly," Aunt Vaney

replied, sort of snappy, as if Dottie Jane had made a request that was not only unheard of but presented ungrammatically.

Dottie Jane mumbled a weak "thank you." Aunt Vaney had drained every bit of fight out of her, I could tell. Just like some big old tree that sucked up all the water so that all the other little trees couldn't have any. But the bigger trees, and the best Christian women, were all closer to heaven, so we had to respect them. Even if it meant we starved to death.

We ate in silence at Vaney's faded yellow kitchen table, our tongues trying to roll over peanut butter that was all oily on the surface and didn't have much taste. I wondered why Aunt Vaney had a kitchen table and chairs at all if she didn't have anyone to gather around at dinnertime, except for crocheted dogs and angels painted on collector plates.

From where I was sitting, I had a clear view of her refrigerator door, where a church calendar was taped perfectly square in the center. Prayer groups and service activities had been starred by hand, and other people's birthdays and anniversaries filled nearly every single box. If you hadn't been up close enough to read the BRIGGS COUNTY BAPTIST header on the top, you might have thought that whoever owned that refrigerator had a very full, very popular month.

I pointed this out to Dottie Jane, and she said that it was sad. Nodding, I acted like I agreed. But really, the calendar scared me. I looked around the bare kitchen, at the floors that were far too polished and the knickknacks with far too few chips, and I wondered if this was the real reward that awaited a Good Christian Woman—to be left alone at the end of your life, after a career of lifting up everybody else, saving everybody else, pushing everyone else forward on the road to full and happy times until they reached the point where they didn't need your prayers anymore. And this was good, because this was your goal for them, and anything else would have been selfish. You'd take your yearly Christmas card, and you'd thank the Lord that the sender's life was too full to bother with calling you more often.

And when you finally died, if you'd done your job exactly right, only God would notice.

DAMAGED GOODNESS

Three hours later, finally out from under the weight of Aunt Vaney's crushing Victorian wallpaper, Dottie Jane and I were perfecting a circus routine on the monkey bars behind our uncle Ron's house. (Well, I was the one putting in all the work on the routine. Dottie Jane was testing the holding power of her home permanent rollers, which were the blue kind. Dottie Jane was sure her mother should have bought the pink kind. It wasn't going to work and that's all there was to it.)

But I was too busy enjoying myself to bother with her complaining, because Uncle Ron and Aunt Joy's house was my favorite to visit out of all the family homes. Most average kids probably wouldn't think so, because Ron and Joy's children were long grown up, so there weren't very many toys still in the house. If you asked for a toy, Joy would give you a choice between everything that was left, which included a doll with one cloudy eye that was all rolled back in its head, a tricycle with no seat, or a Big Wheel that was shaped like a large pink shoe, with no steering wheel. And then, of course, there were the rusted-out monkey bars in the backyard.

I didn't mind any of these things. In fact, I loved having playtime with my cousins that didn't involve them bringing out their five brand-new Cabbage Patch kids while I tried to show off my one, which had green marker drawn on the back of its head. Where there were no new toys to be had, it was a level playing field. Level, except of course for the most creative among us.

"Dottie Jane, pay attention, now," I said, trying my best to picture us in an elegant outdoor amphitheater. I tried to pretend that Meg's and Clayton's screams, which happened approximately every two minutes as the shoe and trike tipped over against the driveway, were some sort of new and fancy percussion.

"It's one ... two ... one ... two ... then you jump back down ..."

The monkey bars were shaped like two side-by-side, upside-down horseshoes with flattened tops. Little bars connected the horseshoes, and you were supposed to grab on to them and swing all the way across with your hands. Neither Dottie Jane nor I could reach these, though, so my entire routine consisted of us going up and down the side ladders at the same time, then performing arabesques when we got to the bottom. If you asked me, it was still pretty spectacular, even if Dottie's arabesques left something to be desired.

"That's silly," she finally said, unrolling a painstakingly wound roller, only to do it up again. It looked a lot messier after she did that.

"Why don't we just go across the top of the bars?" she asked.

"It's too tall. And Momma said not to try it."

Dottie Jane rolled her eyes.

"Maybe for you it's too tall. I take gymnastics."

But you don't take Communion. That's what I was worried about.

Somewhere on the other side of the house, someone endured an especially bloodcurdling wipeout on the pink shoe. It was a sick prelude that only my stomach seemed to hear.

"Dottie Jane, I'm taller than you and I can't even reach . . . I don't think you should . . ."

But I knew that a freight train had not been made that could stop my fifty-pound cousin, driven by her own holy cocktail of root beer, show-offishness, and heavy peroxide.

I watched her jelly shoes bend around each of the thick pipes that made up the ladder. She stood at the top for just a moment, balanced on a thin layer of glitter and plastic that you might have thought was Gibraltar, to look at her face. The top bar looked to be about three feet above her head.

"See, you ca—"

And then the show was over.

The impact knocked the wind out of me, just as if it had happened to my own body. All I could think about was how beautiful Dottie Jane had looked in her midair arabesque, short-lived as it was—one arm reaching desperately toward the top bar, one foot still clinging to the iron bar that was the ladder rung, plastic Miss Clairol rollers silhouetted against the sunset like a laureled crown. If only that nervous little foot had let go.

The strange thing was, Dottie Jane wasn't squalling after the fall. She wasn't making any sound at all. Still wearing a gritted-tooth smile, she was frozen, straddling that iron bar in the exact same posture in which she'd come crashing down on it. Dottie Jane had managed to land on the only part of the worn old monkey bars that had no structural give at all to it.

I looked around quickly to see if a grown-up had been watching, but no one was. This was lucky. Dottie Jane was normally the Queen Squaller of the family, but she and I both knew that if one little sob escaped her mouth this time, we'd spend the rest of the night watching the adults play gin rummy and trying to make that cloudy-eyed doll seem human.

"Here, I'll take care of you," I whispered in her ear, trying to unwind the little legs that she'd now wrapped so tightly around the bar. It was like she was afraid to let go.

Fighting my cousin's little whimpers that threatened to explode any minute, I ran Dottie Jane up the back hill of the house and through the basement door. We crept up the back-stairs and down the hall, into the closest room, the bathroom that was hooked onto my aunt and uncle's bedroom. When we were almost inside, Dottie Jane caught a glimpse of her mother at the end of the hallway, sitting on a living room couch. This was too much for her to bear and I knew it. I managed to shove her inside before the loud part of the wail had escaped. Dottie Jane didn't even seem deterred by the fact that her mother had been asking for a backgammon set; had actually seemed *excited* about the idea of sitting around and playing a dice game for the rest of the night. That could have been our destiny, if I hadn't acted quickly.

"Shhhhh . . ." I tried to soothe her, trying to place her comfortably on the flowered bath mat. "Are you hurt? Are you cut? Is anything . . ."

But before Dottie Jane could answer me, divinity inter-vened. Specifically, my aunt Joy's perfume, which was called "Something Divine," sat in a shimmering, winged bottle on the vanity. It was just the balm Dottie Jane needed.

"Thank goodness!" she cried, snorting the last remnants of the wail back up into her head and leaving not a trace behind. "I needed some of this. I was smelling like those monkey bars."

"Oh. Okay. Are you sure you don't need anything else . . ."

I was rummaging though my uncle's medicine cabinet. But Dottie Jane had found the makeup drawer.

And the Lord shall supply all your needs. Even if they are darn strange.

Once she had applied two or three coats of hand lotion and dusted her face with a powder brush (even though it did not even have any powder on it and didn't seem to make any difference), Dottie Jane declared that she would, indeed, be all right. The only additional therapy she needed was for me to stay behind and entertain her while she went to the bathroom.

I sat down on the edge of the tub and thanked Jesus. Dottie Jane handed me a copy of *Ladies' Home Journal* and asked if I would read her a page that had a picture of some woman yelling at her husband on it. I knew I wasn't supposed to be reading ladies' magazines, but I made an exception. Dottie Jane and I both seemed to be getting away with one of the ultimate summer children's crimes. There would be no splinter, no scar, not even a bruise that anyone could see to mark our disobedience. I flipped to the page and let my body relax with the breeze that was coming in through the little cracked window.

I didn't have time to start reading.

Once again, Dottie Jane didn't scream. She didn't moan and she didn't blink. But as she sat down to do her business, her convicted little eyes grew so quickly that they stopped my mouth from moving. Her tanned face suddenly matched the white bathroom tile.

Dottie Jane moved her shorts aside so that I could see. In the center of her underwear was a tiny drop of blood.

This was too much.

"I'll go get your mom," I said. I started to back out of the bathroom, almost stumbling over myself. Dottie Jane, too, seemed to be moving her rear end as far as possible toward the back of the toilet.

"No. No, no, no, no, no!" she said, over and over again. "I don't want to get in trouble."

"You're hurt, Dottie Jane. I'm getting your mom. You know that you never get in as much trouble if you get hurt. It's only if they find out you did something dangerous and you didn't get hurt. That's when there's trouble."

"No! I said no!" she yelled. I was sure the people in the living room would hear. "I mean I don't want anyone to know. No one can know about this, ever."

"But why—"

"Don't you get it, church girl? My popo bled! It bled by accident. I broke it on the bars. That means I can't . . . I can't get married . . ."

Dottie Jane's words dissolved into a thick puddle of tears. I couldn't make out anything that came from her mouth in the next five minutes, except something about not wanting to have a beehive hairdo. When she'd recovered for a second, she told me that I ought to pad mine, to keep the same thing from happening by accident. She was sure that her own mother kept special pads in the house, and she thought they were for this very purpose. Jesus pads.

"She does not," I said.

"Yes she does! *Yes. She. Does.*" With that last little exclamation, I knew for a fact that Dottie Jane's health was just fine.

But she ended up telling her mother what had happened by the end of the night, anyway. The next day, Aunt Kit took Dottie Jane to the doctor, who said that she'd just broken something that girls didn't need, anyway.

I didn't know what the thing was. I did wonder whether anyone had ever told Aunt Vaney that it was useless.

Lesson 6

For You

Greg and Sharon
Have A
Love Song . . .

To the beat of modern rock or the old favorites, this young couple has a song to sing.

Sometimes it has the hard, driving sound of a restless generation.

Sometimes it has the smooth, mellow sound of yesterday's memories.

Then sometimes it has a reflective, devotional sound that collects thoughts and sheds a brighter light on tomorrow.

Whatever the sound, the song is love . . .

and you should hear it!

Greg and Sharon Hancock are just people who happen to like people. They are fun to be around and have the knack of making a party, a banquet or just a get-together a more pleasurable affair.

Invite a love song to your next gathering. Call Mike at:

Momma and Daddy's brochure from their singing days

Daddy's official Southern Baptist Convention portrait

SOUTHERN BAPTIST CONVENTION
St. Louis, Missouri 1987

Patience

THE BURDEN BOX

To be sure, the whole pagan frog pin incident had left my world feeling off kilter. I did not know quite what to compare the feeling to, but it was close to the same feeling I'd gotten when Daddy showed me how he stayed dry while he was waist-deep in the baptistery. Wading boots. They were kept in a closet behind the baptistery curtain, like a rabbit ready to be pulled from a hat. Except the congregation never saw the rabbit.

I took a lot of satisfaction in adding that fact to my Bible notebook, yet another truth that other kids my age weren't allowed to know. But afterward, part of me wished I didn't have to know it, either. Part of me wanted to keep seeing my father walk right through water; to watch him dance lyrically through pounding, droning hymns, and turn parables of hate and despair into poetry. I wanted to gasp in awe each time he flew out into the mission field with nothing but a prayer on his lips, and no faithless frog talisman whatsoever on his lapel.

I needed to believe in Daddy, and I knew it.

I knew it so thoroughly that it didn't even faze me when, in my second-grade class, we had to go around the room and recite what our daddies did for a living, and Jake Riser hissed "Preacher's kids have problems" when I sat down. What could

I say, he was right, bless his heart. If Jake Riser's father ever broke one of the toilets he was plumbing, he could just fix it. The same went for my classmates' fathers who laid brick, raised cattle, or filled teeth for a living. Everything was repairable or replaceable. And if it wasn't, no one blamed the daddy.

But I knew that if my own father fell from grace—just *once*, that would be all it would take—the damage to souls and saints and heavens that had taken years to polish might be undoable. Even Jake Riser (who, incidentally, was in special-education classes two days a week and probably couldn't read enough gospel to save himself) could see that yes, that would be a problem.

I couldn't let it happen. I *wouldn't* let it happen.

And so I resolved, as God was my witness, that nobody but nobody was going to believe like I did. My light of faith would shine so far and fast that no one could deny it.

Of course, to really get my believing going, I still needed that small element of proof of Daddy's wonder-working power. I had hoped he would just tell me where it lay the night I gave him the frog pin, but that had been a disaster, and I should have seen it coming. Nothing good in my world ever came of demanding "proof" of anything from a grown-up. At best, it sounded like back talk (even though adults demanded proof from us kids all the time, like "show me this" and "add that up"); and at worst, if you were dumb enough to demand it from an adult like Mrs. Mounts, it sounded like a sin. (Mrs. Mounts had nearly washed Meg's little mouth out with soap the day she asked why God didn't invent the camera earlier, so that Jesus could just take pictures of Himself to leave behind for nonbelievers.)

If I really wanted to know Daddy's secret, I was going to have to search it out for myself. This was not a daunting prospect, given that I had a pretty good idea of where it might be kept.

Like all revered pastors, my daddy had a study in the church. It was pretty much the only room in the building that rivaled the sanctuary in terms of fanciness and shine, and it was just as filled with light. Sunbeams seemed to skip right over the heads of wandering souls on the streets outside, play xylophone-like down the wall plaques commemorating many acts of humble soul saving, bounce off the brass desk set, and, finally, electrify the blinding teeth of the pastor's daughters, framed in perfect obedience behind their father's head. Even the ebony tribesmen figures Daddy had brought back from the missions effort to Nigeria glowed sun-white under mile-thick coats of Miss Frankie's furniture wax.

Surely no common penitent, stumbling from that office half blinded by the light, his nostrils baptized raw with Pine-Sol (which Miss Frankie called "Southern Baptist Incense"), would have guessed that Daddy's true lair of holiness was somewhere else entirely. Somewhere deeper and darker and closely guarded, where even Mrs. Mounts couldn't sniff out the nuclear force of prayer and pastorizing that went on inside.

Yes, my daddy's home basement study was the Batcave of General Drive.

But while Daddy had the holiest secret subterranean lair by far, he did not have the only one. Nearly every daddy of every neighbor kid I knew seemed to have some sort of a hideout in the family basement. Nate Davis's father had a little shop set up where he hand-painted Civil War soldier figurines and squinted into a magnifying glass with such determination that it suffocated out all his other senses. (He never even seemed to hear when Nate's momma hollered at the top of her lungs that he needed to come up and look at some leak or some smell or some noise.) The Stinsons' daddy had a bench and a bunch of dumbbells way off in a basement corner. And Keith Taylor's father, way out at the end of the street, beneath a house where my mother seemed to never want Meg and me to spend too much time, had a marvelous collection of cans and an old VCR where he replayed the same Reds games from three seasons ago over and over and over.

Not that I thought this was strange. Where I lived, it was common knowledge that mommas held strict court over the sunlit, potpourri-scented upstairs living quarters of our street. But the daddies held sway over the basements.

They had to share them with us kids, of course. Everything that was too rowdy, too grass-stained, or too unstarched to set foot at street level had to find refuge in the basements, too, and that usually included the children of the house. But we never ventured into our fathers' reserved corners. We only tiptoed around them with great fear and reverence for our mothers' stairtop instruction—"You stay clear of Dad down there. He's *relaxing!*" (It wasn't until years later that I realized *relaxing* actually meant "unwinding." The dire warning that was snapped into that word by every momma I ever knew, and especially my own, had me convinced that *relaxing* was the equivalent of "calibrating fragile nuclear devices.")

No, I knew that to venture into Daddy's special study area, I would need special permission. That, or circumstances specially arranged for me by the only Father higher than my own.

The day those circumstances were graced upon my shoulders was also a day that I was reminded that the Lord could, indeed, make holy uses out of my little sister.

It happened on the evening of the First Monday of July. Now, at my house, the First Monday night of the month was "Momma's High Holy Night," or so she called it. Daddy always had a Western Sizzlin' dinner with the church trustees on those evenings, and they were the only church functions to which my momma, sister, and I were not invited. To make up for the snub, Momma always really made over us on that night. We were allowed to cook a frozen pizza in the oven, then eat it on an old sheet spread out on the living room floor, picnic-style. It was our own private celebration, and before eating we always said a prayer to forgive all fathers who dined elsewhere, for they knew not what they were missing.

As it turned out, though, the end of that particular First Monday dinner had me longing for the civility of the Western Sizzlin'. I squinted across the living room to the couch, where Meg was once again laid out—snoring, sweating, and "separated for *one hour*" at Momma's command.

Well, of course she is, I thought. *Separated by the pure grace of Jesus, and we are loath to tolerate her.*

In my opinion, anyone who had behaved in such a manner over our pizza dinner certainly lacked the grace to carry her own tray in Kentucky's most prestigious steak house. Meg would surely have dropped spaghetti in the salad dressing in the buffet line. She'd have tried to grab the elegant waitress's perfect cowboy hat. She would have embarrassed our family, and therefore made the whole church seem on unsolid footing. That's why the trustees had issued their "church gentlemen only" rule for the fancy First Monday Dinners, I decided. It was for Margaret Gates Hancock's sake.

And a little child shall spoil it for everybody else. That ought to be the First Commandment.

Midway between my sister and me on the floor, near where Momma was crouched over some of her classroom posters, sat a plastic McDonaldland dinner plate that had once been part of a two-plate set. Meg had (of course) ruined her own plate the week before by using it as a flying disk in the backyard. Yet when First Monday Dinner came around, she thought she could just march right up and claim the plate that I had managed to keep pristine. Now her greed was ruining the night for everyone. Or so it appeared at first.

"Hmmm . . . his one needs more yellow," Momma mused, oblivious once again to the great injustice. "Em, can you run downstairs to Daddy's study? See if he's got any markers in the top drawer of his desk?"

For a moment I didn't move. I just sat on the edge of the wingback chair and forgot to breathe out. Surely, I thought, she'd think better of her request that I venture into one of the "parents only" parts of our house. And Daddy's private pastoral study, at that.

I squirmed a little on the edge of the cushion, fending off the disappointment that I knew would come. She'd come to her senses as soon as the marker odor dissipated.

Go look in Daddy's top desk drawer. Sure, Emy, you're that lucky.

Momma might as well have asked me to go dump out her bedside table cabinet, throw open her silk makeup case, and rummage through the bill drawer in the kitchen all at once. This had to be either a dream or a trick. A go-out-and-play-on-the-neighbors'-trampoline, but-I'm-going-to-come-out-there-in-a-minute-and-tell-you-I-thought-better-of-it-so-you-have-to-get-off kind of a thing. Momma had done that before. Several times, actually. And yet she wondered what made Meg and me so exceptionally prone to temptation.

I wouldn't have minded if she thought better of it this time, because I liked watching Momma do her class bulletin boards. I often wished some of my own Bible School teachers had the same passion for crinkle border and cardboard letters as my momma, a Michelangelo with tempera. Most of the King's Way Baptist Sunday School teachers didn't even bother to decorate their classrooms at all, except for putting up an illustration or two torn straight out of *HomeLife*, and not even caring enough to cut off the jagged edge on top. (Now who, I ask you, could feel the *weightiness* of God's miracles when they were hung up there cockeyed with a pitiful little piece of Scotch Tape?)

Thank heaven, Sharon Hancock could never be one of those. If she had, I might have lost my one chance at a glimpse inside Daddy's secret temple. But as it was, she was too busy attacking that posterboard like a master canvas to think twice about her request.

I tried my best to tiptoe out of the room and down the basement steps without making a squeak.

The basement felt cooler, lighter than the rest of the house. Lighter than the rest of the world. Black as it was, something within it felt as strong and tough and comforting as the finest of King's Way Baptist's pews. Unlike the pews, though, it was dirty and gritty underneath my feet, and it held up our whole house without creak or comment because that was what it was made to do. It didn't need to look, or smell, or be Pine-Solled as if it needed to do anything else. Maybe that was why Daddy liked it, I decided. Maybe that was why all daddies liked the basement.

My only thought when I pulled the light chain inside the study's door was that it was a good thing this was not the particular pastor's office that was located inside the church building. Because Miss Frankie, even bolstered by a weekend army of Women's League volunteers, was way too frail to survive cleaning *this*.

Between me and what I supposed was Daddy's desk, about twenty thousand tons of spiritual-life refuse had settled at the bottom of our house. There were stacks of to-be-written church cards scattered everywhere, like little land mines Daddy avoided as he paced around his peaceful little niche. He'd once told me how he secretly coded each card for the occasion—the baby-lamb card was for baptisms; the candle-and-cross card was for old-person birthdays; the rising sun was for sorry-about-your-job; the clasped hand was for sorry-about-your grandma; and the biggest, most shiny card of all, with the foil sunrise and poem in calligraphy, was for sorry-you're-still-mad-about-last-week's-sermon.

There was lots of incoming mail, too. Lots of thank-yous in the form of homemade jam that smelled faintly of mold, and electric silk Jesus ties that I thought were beautiful but that Daddy always said (mumbling toward the floor, probably out of humility) were "too nice not to save for a really special occasion."

There was plenty of nonchurch clutter in there, too. Daddy's sneakers and his boots and yard shoes were all knotted together in a pile in the middle of the floor. I could swear that I saw a pair of his good preaching shoes at the bottom, like all the heathen-life shoes had ganged up and suffocated them.

There were stacks of seminary books as tall as Meg, all piled up so that the big old dowdy volumes crushed the newer books with the prettier covers and holographic crosses.

But despite all the mess, I had to say, one thing I did not have to avoid in Daddy's study was dust. There were lots of old things, lots of out-of-style things, and lots of papers and pages and volumes that were so worn out they were almost see-through. But all the dust in the basement study was in the air. None of it seemed to be able to settle in the place where my father planned and worshipped. It danced in little swirls and spirals through the ribbons of light that cut through the tiny window at the top of the wall, as if it knew it had better not settle down. You always had to be on watch in a preacher's house. Even the littlest things could sense that. *Especially* the littlest things could sense it.

I pulled open the top drawer of Daddy's desk with all the fear and skill of Indiana Jones. A tiny cobweb, one that would have been imperceptible to anyone but a child with the sensation of disobedience on her fingertips, drifted down from the ceiling and brushed my bare shoulder. I jumped. The distinctive creak of Momma's weight echoed directly above my head. *Oh no.* Was she pausing? She could feel my true motive through the floorboards, I just knew it.

Swallowing the fear, I reminded myself how important this duty of discovering, this duty of believing, was. It was something Momma wouldn't understand. Not that she didn't want to; she just didn't *need to* like I did. Sharon Hancock was a pillar of faith. She'd outgrown her need-to-knows like I was outgrowing my newest pair of sandals.

I held my breath and dug into the drawer.

At first, I didn't see anything special. It looked like a regular adult's desk drawer, all crammed full of more markers and pens than any one grown-up could ever hope to use but no kid was ever allowed to color with. There were tracts and pennies and postage stamps, and the stickers Daddy gave me for practicing my handwriting. There was even the pair of Momma's kitchen shears that she'd been looking for for more than a year, though I opted to overlook this apparent sin. This mission was about uncovering the key to Daddy's saintliness, and nothing else. *Something* had to be here.

And then I saw it. There, underneath the very yellow Magic Marker Momma had asked me to recover, was a little silver key.

I lifted it to the light, slowly and reverently, embracing every detail so that I could write about it later, when called upon by Him to record the miracle in my Bible notebook. Where there was a key, there had to be a locked something nearby. *Now where was that . . .*

And then I remembered. *Of course!* I had seen it from the corner of my eye the handful of times I'd been allowed in the study for a minute only, to kiss Daddy good night or to take his empty coffee cup up for a wash. Right inside the door, on a humble shelf made of concrete blocks and two-by-fours, was a small locked box. That had to be it. The Ark of the Preacher Daddy.

"Uh . . . the what of the *what*, little lady?"

I'd been so overcome with the miracle of discovery that

I hadn't realized I was talking out loud. In fact, all my senses must have shut off in that moment, because I hadn't even heard Daddy walk up directly behind me.

"I–I was supposed to get a marker for Momma. She said I could come down here," I stammered.

I thought for a moment that I might be able to conceal the key and slip it back on the desk unnoticed. But I gripped it so hard that it slipped out of my hand and tinkled on the floor. *Pieces of silver always tell the tale, Emy. You ought to know that.*

I couldn't even look up at Daddy, but I swore I felt his anger spread through the dust in the air. The clanging of that key just kept on echoing back and forth in my head.

"Miss Em, were you snooping through your daddy's private things?" he asked.

The *yes, sir* came out barely ahead of the tears. I still couldn't raise my head. I might have talked my way out of this by quoting scripture to Mrs. Mounts, or talking miracles to Momma. Maybe. But my soul did not dare deem itself worthy to take on my father. I waited for his final word of punishment—the proclamation, the absolution, the Amen that would let me walk upright out of the room again.

But when he spoke again, I heard a smile at the edge of his voice.

"Well, honey, I wish you'd just *asked* . . ."

When I finally did look up (with one eye open just in case it wasn't over, as was my habit from praying in church), Daddy wasn't even looking at me, much less looking at me angrily. He was turned toward the bookshelf, lifting the Ark from its pedestal. In a single motion he carried it over to his desk chair, where he sat and patted his knee, as if I should sit down.

"You really want to see what's in here?" he asked.

I nodded more quickly than was necessary, out of embarrassment. I hoped to shake the pre-punishment tears back into my head.

It didn't fool Daddy. He rolled his eyes and threw a glance at the ceiling that said *they know not what they do* louder than words.

"Well, give me that key, then."

I handed the key to Daddy and took my seat on his lap. With the benefit of all my senses back in play again, I could hear Momma and Meg running about upstairs. I still hoped neither of them would come down. Even though I had clear permission to be where I was now, something made me feel like a moment was coming that wasn't for them to share.

"This," Daddy said, turning the box upside down as he fumbled with the key from all angles, "is something I made in junior high wood shop. The lock isn't much good. Come to think of it, I don't know why I even try to use it, but I always do . . ."

After a few more twists, Daddy let out a big breath and dropped the box on his lap. I heard temptation incarnate shuffle around inside, but the lock hadn't budged.

"Well, maybe it just isn't going to open for us tonight," he said. "I'll tell you about it later, honey. Why don't you go on up to bed."

Daddy patted me quickly on the behind. I felt him start to rise from the chair himself, but I grasped the arm in spite of myself and held firm.

"Miss Em, now don't be—"

"Can I try it, Daddy? Just once, let me try the lock. Please?"

I pleaded. I knew it was pitiful of me, but I was *so* close to getting the truth. "Please, I just . . . I really want to try it. You made it and I think it's neat!"

For as long as I could, I sat there gripping the box, holding up the practiced gaze that had helped me evade bedtime more than once. As usual, I planned to stop this as soon as the look on Daddy's face shifted from exhaustion to irritation. But this time, I didn't see either look cross his face. There was something different that had settled in Daddy's blue-gray eyes. It was not an unfamiliar look, but it seemed out of place.

Finally, it clicked—it was the expression Daddy had the first day he let me ride my bicycle without him beside me; the look that was there again on the first day he put me on the bus to school.

Daddy wasn't tired of the box in my hands; he was afraid of it. He was afraid of it, and he knew that I could see it. I watched his eyes lower, and he traced the wooden corners again.

After a minute, Daddy let out an awkward little giggle.

"It's just a crummy old class project that I kept around for God only knows why," he said. "Go ahead and open it; you'll be disappointed."

Daddy should have had no reason to swallow—*hard*—as he handed over the box and key, but he did.

With just a couple of quick turns in the lock, the lid sprang open so easily it almost hit my chin. It hadn't been stuck at all.

Daddy didn't make a move or say anything, so I just started talking. It felt like one of those situations a kid runs into sometimes, where adults are talking and you don't know about what, but you feel the drive to do something kid-like and silly to change the subject. Even though you do not yet know what the subject is.

"Does it play music?" I babbled. "Because Grandy has a box kind of like this, but it's musical and Memaw gave it to him, and this one sort of looks like . . ."

I kept talking, as Daddy carefully lifted a folded handkerchief that covered the contents of the box.

To look at it, the stuff in the box looked just about as non-special as the box itself. There was an old bow tie and set of cuff links, a handful of little Army pins and patches, one or two black-and-white pictures, and a couple of letters with runny ink. It might as well have been Momma's upstairs junk drawer. But Momma didn't handle the household junk like Daddy handled each trinket in the box, weighing it carefully in each hand, as if it were as sacred as the bread and wine.

I watched Daddy carefully lay each treasure on his lap. I wasn't sure how much time passed as he refolded each letter, flattened each patch as if to iron it, and shined each cuff link in slow circles with his shirttail. In my mind, this might have only taken seconds, but by the time he was finished, the sun had faded beyond the window, and all the dancing dust had calmed and bowed out of sight, until it was just the light from the ceiling bulb that encircled the two of us.

Finally, Daddy spoke. But this time, it was him who kept his head bowed.

"Well, there," he said. "So which do you want to know about?"

His tone made me think I could pick only one—or maybe it was me who only *wanted* to pick one—so I studied the objects carefully. Finally, I laid my finger on one of the folded letters. It was addressed in a careful script, like Momma's.

Daddy swallowed again, almost so small I couldn't see it. But it was there. He picked up the letter as if it were the last remaining piece of papyrus written by one of his ancient prophets.

"This," he said, fingering the edge of the envelope but not opening it. "This is a letter to your mom and me from Susie Delacroix."

I didn't know the name.

"Is she a friend?" I asked.

"She was." Daddy nodded. "Was a real good friend of ours."

He told me about the great Susie Delacroix, a Bluegrass horsewoman whose heart outgalloped every steed she ever rode. She'd gone to church with my mother and father, eaten dinner with them afterward, taken all her nourishment from the Hancock family pulpit and plate, and left the greatest laugh and the wildest stories you'd ever heard behind as tip.

Every now and then as he talked, I could tell that Daddy was pausing against his will, remembering. With a nod or a quick question, I would urge him forward.

Daddy barely paused for breath when he got to the part where Susie was thrown from her horse during a practice. She was thrown and she landed on a metal farm tool someone had left behind in an open field. There was a lot of blood and there was nothing anyone could do. He said it just like that, fast and plain at the end. And then he didn't say anything else for a long time.

The silence threatened to take over, as Susie Delacroix's death hung in midair between my father and me. He looked different through that air, somehow, even though I'd stood by his side next to about a hundred caskets, and held his hand at half a dozen vigils.

But my father had never before described to me what

happened in the time before the funerals, when he was always called in to do the last he could for a member of his dear congregation who was moving from this earth. He'd never described for me how it was when someone died; someone he'd baptized or married. I wondered how many awful details, how many moans and stains and last gasps for prayer were resting somewhere behind the lines of his forehead.

"Di-did you cry, Daddy?"

It was a dumb-kid question, but it was all I could whisper. He raised his head and looked straight at me, and suddenly Susie, and all the tears left behind in the wake of her last gallop, seemed to drift to the basement of his thoughts. Suddenly Daddy was just as composed as if the box had never been opened.

"No, sweetie," he said. "No, I didn't cry. I couldn't."

"Couldn't?"

I barely managed to push the word out, past the fog of confusion that now hung around the man I'd known longer than any in my life. Any hope I'd once held of finding out how he reconciled his holy and regular selves seemed completely shot to heck. This was the man who spent every third Thursday in our living room with the Widows' Group, repeating "It's okay to cry" like a shaman summoning the rains, praying and soothing and harmonizing with the falling tears like they were his own angelic chimes. This same man was now telling me that, in fact, crying was against all his rules.

Worse, I knew that this time there was probably no question I could ask that would clear things up, that would finally get me a satisfying answer about how my daddy worked. If I ran to Momma and told her what he'd just said, she'd tell me something like, *Well, it's supposed to seem like that with daddies and their children. Daddies are supposed to seem larger than life, and you're not supposed to understand how they work.* Maybe. Maybe other daddies. Maybe the ones whose daily business wasn't a storefront full of "understanding."

"No . . . ," Daddy went on. He neatly refolded the patches and letters from the box.

". . . when you're a preacher, the crying's just not in the job description. You have to keep everything running, keep everything together when something tragic happens. So that other people can cry. So that they can have *their* moment."

"But that's not fair!" I interrupted. I couldn't put a finger on why this thing poked uncomfortably at me. The only feeling I could compare it to was the one that rose up in my chest every time I saw my mother put back a dress she'd wanted in the Hearst's Department Store. She'd look at the price tag once, twice, three times. Then she'd put it back on the rack, swallow hard, and leave the store like she was almost proud to have left behind the thing she wanted so badly.

"It's fair," he said. "Everybody gives something up. The 'getting to cry' is just the thing I gave up."

Daddy put all the medals and letters back inside the box, and I helped him relock it and rebrush all the dust off the top, even though there really wasn't any. And after a while, I looked him in the eye again and I nodded. I nodded a nod that meant what it was supposed to mean. I understood. I understood, and for the sake of my own shame, I wished I didn't. My daddy'd never get a medal, like the cop on TV who gave up his life to block a bullet meant for someone else. He'd never get the president's handshake, like a soldier who gave up a leg so that his country could be protected. But he did give up almost every emotional experience that makes being human worthwhile so that others would have an unburdened chance to experience it for themselves.

All for the glory of God. It didn't seem like enough.

At the very least, it was deserving of more than a daughter who was sometimes embarrassed to tell kids at school that her father preached for a living. Who'd actually hidden out in the bathroom the day he was asked to come pray over our school's Thanksgiving Dinner Pageant. Sure, I was the top dog at King's Way Baptist on Sunday mornings, but outside, I was on my own. Outside, I had every bit of Judas's confidence in my daddy, and now I knew it. Now I knew that it was me who had the holy and nonholy selves that needed reconciling, not him.

How could I have actually turned red-faced when Jake Riser sneered at me? Of *course* preachers' kids had problems. How could you not, when your daddy had to keep all his worldly burdens locked in a box on the basement shelf? Jake's daddy might have cried out all drunken in the street two nights a week, but at least he could cry out. At least he could cry out.

LONG-HAIRED PROPHETS

The truth of Daddy's burdens hit me so hard that I couldn't speak. I tried to swallow and collect myself, but before I knew it, Daddy's good First Monday Dinner shirt had a puddle spreading over the left shoulder and down the top of the sleeve.

He took out a handkerchief (which he always did for distressed people, though it was silly because everyone just ignored it and cried all over him anyway). And then he began to laugh.

"Well, Miss Em! Now, now, somebody's getting all moved by the spirit again too close to bedtime. Your mother'll kill me for letting you get all riled up like this."

I was trying to tell him I was sorry, for the embarrassment and the shame and all of it, but the sobs and the snot clogged up my nose so much that all the words came out jumbled together. Daddy just smoothed my hair and patted my back until my breathing came into a normal rhythm again. He was just about better at that than anybody in the world, I decided. Doctors might be able to stop the pain, but they couldn't get rid of the tears like that.

"There now, honey," he whispered. "You calmed down enough to go on to bed?"

I knew Daddy could probably still feel my heart racing

through my back, so I opted not to lie. I shook my head. The truth was, I knew I was going to have to deal with visions of dead Susie Delacroix long after the lights went out.

"Here," he said, lifting me off his lap as he stood and walked toward the shelf. "Now, if you want to know my real pastor's secret—and that is what you came down here for, correct? Well, let me just show you . . ."

I grinned a stupid grin and waited until Daddy was facing the bookshelf before I ran up behind him fast enough to make Bruce Jenner jealous.

Daddy was thumbing through his old record collection. I peered closer around his elbow, searching for whatever it was he'd hidden behind the vinyl. But there didn't seem to be anything on the shelves except Daddy's old albums.

"Here," he said, holding one album out in front of him by the very edges, as if the light had to catch the cardboard cover just right for its true beauty to be revealed.

". . . this," he went on, rubbing the cover carefully, "this is what keeps my soul calmed down and on point."

Daddy held up the album in front of me, lifting it with both his hands and his smile, as if I was supposed to be amazed and enlightened just to be in the presence of some moldy old record.

"It doesn't look like church music," I told him, crossing my arms.

"Well, not church music, no. But spiritual music, Lord have mercy, yes it is."

I craned my neck sideways and squinted at Daddy's relic. It was burgundy-colored with gold writing at the top—a little like a pew Bible, I supposed. And on the cover, four men with long, bushy hair and mustaches might well have been some stranded apostles on a detour. But I doubted it.

Still, I tried to play along. It was getting later, and Daddy had already obliged me more bedtime reprieve than I had ever had.

"Matthew, Mark, Luke, and John?" I wondered. "The soundtrack from the Easter Pageant?"

"Ooohh, blasphemy!" Daddy laughed, punching me lightly on the arm. "No, this is Crosby, Stills, Nash, and Young."

He quickly stifled the smile, dropped to his knees next to me, and prayed aloud, solemn as could be but in a big goofball voice: "Forgive me, Father, for I have neglected to teach the gospel to my own daughter."

Now, this was getting to be a little too much. I'd come to unravel my father's secrets, and I had, but now the great mysticism of the basement was wearing off, fast. But before I could remind Daddy of how close to my bedtime it really was, he had launched into a sermon that forced every little bit of a yawn back into my belly.

"You see, kid—and don't you ever tell Memaw this—but I've never opened a single one of her *Great Hymns of the Ages* albums. She shoves them underneath my Christmas stocking every year, and they're sitting wrapped in the plastic they came in, locked in the bottom drawer of that file cabinet. Now that key, you'll *never* find." He laughed. He took my hand and ran it slowly over the wave of multicolored album spines that lined the old rickety shelf, as if he were having me inspect fine linen that had been locked away for ages in a forgotten vault. He kept on talking, but now and then he'd close his eyes, like he could just feel their melodies through the cardboard and the hush.

"Now this," he said. "*This* is what keeps me going. People just singing about what keeps their hearts beating, what keeps them sane. Where they put their troubles; where they count their blessings."

"And Memaw doesn't know how to count her blessings?" I said, wide-eyed. I was really throwing this "question" in for show. My favorite part of any talk with Daddy was the part where I played dumb and challenged him. A preacher has to be prepared to meet the lowliest member of his flock right where she stands, after all. At least that was what Memaw always said as she got us ready to deliver school supplies at the poor people's community center.

"No, no." Daddy took the bait. "No, that's not what I meant. It's just that, well . . . Miss Em, people like Memaw never quite understood how the church and rock and roll could mix. They never quite got the beat and they never will. But man, in the middle of all those throbbing pipe organs, and choir women screeching about blood and thorns and slaughtered lambs . . . it just gets you so hyped up and scared and numb that you can't hear in there, you know?

"I don't know how I could explain it any better," he went on, "to you or to your grandmother or anyone else. I just think somewhere in the middle of all of it, the peace got lost. We got so busy yelling at people about where they ought to find it that we drowned it out."

I nodded like I understood, but the truth was that I didn't want to, and was afraid to, just yet. Daddy was wearing the look adults also got when they realized their child was going to lose the very thing they had lost once.

"But you haven't lost it, have you, Daddy?" I comforted

him, smoothing out David Crosby's hair on the album cover like he was my father's own disgruntled doll.

"Nope." Daddy half smiled again. "Give me a slow acoustic guitar solo from one of the greats any day. No bass, no chord played so hard it jumps inside your rib cage. Just let me hear it flow, natural as breathing. 'Cause mark my words, Miss Em. If I die one day, and I end up in a place where the man in charge sounds like some belching pipe organ that time forgot, I'll know I made a heck of a wrong turn somewhere."

And then, with the unique sort of head bow I only saw him employ at his Sunday benedictions, Daddy slid the album out of its cover and onto our old record player. Low as a prayer, David Crosby tiptoed into my father's holy lair like he'd always been waiting there, behind the stacks of seminary texts.

You, who are on the road, must have a code, that you can live by . . .

While the record played low in the background, Daddy took me on a tour of the framed black-and-white pictures— some photos, some clipped for newspapers—that lined space in the wall above the album shelves. I'd never noticed them before; they just blended into the old fake-wood paneling, which was scarred all over with pushpin holes.

Some of the pictures were from concerts—Momma and Daddy, hair of the same length brushing each other's shoulders, arm in arm with my Uncle Hal and Aunt T, in front of some stage that looked a mile away.

But in most of the pictures, the stage was closer. In those pictures, framed, standing for all time in the spotlight, Sharon

Rae and Gregory Lee Hancock, just out of college and so in love it made the paper wrinkle, belted out their souls to every VFW, roller rink, and church rec hall from here to Tennessee. All the while, singing old-time gospel that didn't have one bit of "old time" about it.

I had heard about this, from people in the church who pinched my cheeks and told me that they knew my mother and father "from the time when they used to sing." But that always seemed like something out of another testament altogether—a whole set of books that you were supposed to study and to know, but that you couldn't act out in the present day, because they were in a language no one could remember anymore. My mother, in her old testament, had hair that wasn't short. My father rode a motorcycle. They played and they sang to a God who didn't have arthritis, like the one I worshipped did, creaking thunderclaps every time He rose up to smite someone. It was as if Momma and Daddy'd lived a whole life before.

. . . and so, become yourself, because the past, is just a good-bye . . .

But looking at the display on the study wall, that life didn't seem entirely gone. Here and there, old tickets and programs were stuck into the corners of picture frames, almost as if someone thought they might end up being useful again. One frame even held an entire poster, with Momma and Daddy in second billing to Grady Nutt, a Christian comedian whom I couldn't remember very well, but who had been to our house a few times between his weekly spots on *Hee Haw*, where he played a country preacher.

The prayer Daddy had written for Grady's funeral, just a few days after his small touring plane crashed onto a runway in

Alabama, was folded into a corner of the old wooden burden box, alongside Dad's tears for Susie Delacroix.

. . . their father's hell . . . did surely go by . . .

But inside their shining picture frames nailed high above the box, there was no sense of burden on my parents' faces. They laughed and smiled there for eternity, praying for nothing more substantial than enough coins in the tip jar to pay for gas money home. No pipe organ required. I could tell from the sparkle in their eyes that neither one of them dared imagine a time when life would be heavy enough to require the rocket-boosting power of a pipe organ.

"Yeah, we were something else, weren't we?" Daddy said, beaming. And not just at me, it seemed. He stood there with his hands on his hips, reveling, just a few feet away from where a slightly bent music stand and a dented box marked TOURING JACKETS, BELL-BOTTOMED BRITCHES seemed to pick up part of his glow.

"Why aren't you still doing that?" I asked him. "I mean you and Momma. Why aren't you still singing on the road? You could have been famous!"

I thought for a minute that I ought not to have added the part about Daddy maybe being famous. There is no higher calling than that of a minister, of course. Of course I knew that.

But he didn't even seem to consider the question. He just laughed and rattled off the reply like a memory verse—like he had it saved up in the event of that very question, because he knew his own salvation depended on repeating it a hundred times.

"Well, honey, the best I can say is, sometimes the road to the cross is easier than the road to Hollywood."

"Really?" I asked. I had half expected him to add, *Proverbs Something: Something* at the end of the thought.

"Oh yes, really." He laughed again. "I don't regret it one bit, if that's what you're wondering. Lots of us from the old rock-and-roll bands ended up going the pastoral route because it was an easier way to be onstage and inspire people. Just another way to move souls, when you get right down to it. Plus a warm bed and a salary at the end of every night. It beats the back of a tour bus. And who knows, somebody might just escape eternal damnation if you have a good performance."

Daddy picked up an old photo album with guitar picks glued to the front in a star shape.

"I wasn't the only one, you know," he said, pulling apart the stuck pages. "Best bass player I ever knew is behind a pulpit in Birmingham. The best drummer ... Lord, last I heard he was driving a missions bus door-to-door through the Appalachians. Come to think of it, I bet there's not a preacher you'd find alive today who didn't once dream of a life under a big spotlight."

"And when did they all stop the dreaming?" I asked.

"Oh, I wouldn't say stopped. Eventually, I guess all of us realized that there was a different kind of stage on every corner in America, a lot closer to home. And there, the fans hang on for dear life, you know? Now, get on up to bed; I mean it."

I hugged Daddy's leg and bounded up the basement stairs, stepping so fast and light that I barely made a squeak. To tell the truth, I was more excited about getting out of the basement than I had been to finally go down into it. I knew that I didn't belong there. I knew that my daddy didn't want me to belong there. It was the place where my father kept the reminders of everything he'd sacrificed to be Daddy to me; to be father to a whole town.

It was the place where burdens had sunk to the bottom. But they would never go away. Preachers wouldn't be in business if they did.

THE MISSAL LAUNCH

All up and down General Drive, the germ angel had been experiencing its most generous giving season to date, bestowing chicken pox on each of my neighbors. Yet though I had prayed in earnest for two months after my visit to Mary Anna Stinson's front porch, I did not share in their affliction. Betty Claremore's holy fame seemed a world away.

It pained me to think about how wretchedly awful every one of my neighbor children was at handling that God-given disease. Forget about using it to draw others to His glory. No, when Mrs. Taylor opened the front door so that Momma could deliver my get-well card to her little boy Keith (Momma made me stand way back and wave from the edge of the driveway), Keith waved back at me. But in the process of lowering his hand back down, he managed to scratch his head, pick his nose, and rub an open patch of sores on his arm in one fell swoop. Now how, I ask you, could anyone help but lose their appetite for the blessed bread of life after they saw *that*?

Had I stood in Keith's mismatched slippers, I knew exactly what I would have done when a guest called. I would have made sure I was dressed in my best pajamas and kept my head low under my burden. And when the person calling to pay respects said, "I bet you can't wait to get rid of those itchy sores"

I would have said, "Oh no, ma'am, it is a privilege. For I have taken on the pox of the world so that you and your unwashed children may be itch-free." Then all the countless marathons, can drives, and cookie sales would be held in my honor. And of course, Christ the Lord's.

But it didn't look like I was going to get my chance to be a pox martyr. Once or twice I was sure that it was happening, but then Momma told me that the bumps on my forearm and face were hives, and said I ought to settle down out of whatever it was I was getting so worked up about.

I had to make sure the lines of communication between the Lord Jesus and myself were clear and direct. Because so far He wasn't hearing a gosh-darn thing, over the squalls on my block that arose like a nightly alarm, as gallons of hydrogen peroxide were applied simultaneously. I needed to get His attention fast, and I decided that I would have to humble myself to do it. I would take Mary Anna's advice, however stuck-up and strange, and I would pray over a missal for a powerful (but temporary) affliction.

This posed a problem, because I was quite sure such an object would never make its way into my house. That is, unless it was mixed in with one of Mrs. Mounts's monthly deliveries to my father of "things she'd located through various sources" that were "a danger to the spiritual welfare of our children." But those monthly shoe-box-fuls usually consisted of nothing more than some old tapes, some magazines with naked ladies on the front, and whatever new brand of overly caffeinated cola was in the front window of the Dairy Mart. I hadn't seen anything like the small, strange book Mary Anna had held out before me.

There was only one thing to do. I would search our house for the closest thing to a Baptist missal that I could find. And if I couldn't find one, I'd make my own darn missal.

This would be a tough task, because I didn't have a lot to go on as far as knowledge of what a missal was supposed to look and feel like. Naturally, I had tried to avert my eyes from that object as much as possible while Mary Anna brandished it like a sword at my throat. But I knew that it was small and square, and just about as thick as it was wide. And, as Mary Anna had said, it was full of prayers, and when her momma prayed over it, "things" happened.

I mulled this idea of a missal over and over in my mind the night before I actually began my search for one, and I found that it made me too nervous to sleep. The more I thought about what it was and what it was supposed to do, the more it sounded like a spell book. Like the kind of book I heard Momma say had been taken away from some kids up at the high school after they were caught out in the parking lot chanting with safety pins stuck in their faces. I wondered if maybe that was why the female members of the Stinson household never came out of the house. Maybe they were in there most of the time wandering around with safety pins in their faces. Maybe what I had thought was the smell of bleach wafting out onto their porch was actually rubbing alcohol, to clean all the pinpricks.

I decided then and there that I had better not ask my mother or daddy to help me find a missal. No, it was better that they not know what I was getting involved in at *all*. It was funny, I thought, how at our church all anyone ever talked about was what would happen if you didn't pray hard enough. No one ever said what could happen if you prayed too much, or too well. Maybe that was what the Catholics talked about during their Sunday Masses. Maybe that was why almost all the Catholics I'd ever met seemed so scared, so often. They knew what could happen with one powerful, one out-of-control prayer.

The next day, while Daddy was mowing the grass, I went to search his bookshelves for something missal-like. Not surprisingly, he didn't have anything like that. I hoped God's answer to my request was somewhere else in the house.

And wouldn't you know it, this time He came to me again in the privacy of the bathroom. I could not for the life of me figure out why He kept choosing this location. It certainly didn't have anything to do with privacy. Every time my sister or I took longer than ten seconds to use the toilet, Momma was opening up the door and asking if everything was okay and could she bring us a book.

This was the thought I was having when I looked in the mirror over the sink and glimpsed the small stack of books that had accumulated on the back of the toilet. Most of them were Meg's, as she was littler and the brunt of Momma's "book treatment" had passed down to her. But right on top of the stack was one that I had not wanted to hand down yet.

It was my book of rhyming poems and prayers. Someone had given it to me when I was a baby. But of course I couldn't read it then, so it got placed on the highest shelf in my nursery, where Momma put all of the gifts that were "most special," meaning, highly inappropriate for a newborn. One day, while Momma was dusting and I was playing on my pallet, it had fallen to the floor like a ton of bricks. And according to Momma, something in my teething gums had taken to the thick, cardboard pages of that book like it was balm from above.

The book had a delicate little painting on the front of a little girl looking out into a starry night. You could tell just by the cover, I thought, that it was meant only for very sophisticated, very prayerful children, because in all other kiddie books, the kids on the covers looked like goony cartoon characters, with oversize heads and tongues lolling out of their mouths.

That little girl on the cover looked like she might—just might—pass for one of the angels I'd seen painted on the cover of Mary Anna's missal.

The book wasn't quite missal-thick, but it was sturdy enough for Meg to have once substituted it for a brick in one of her building sets. The spine was plain and not engraved fancy at all (another good sign), and it was made of cloth. The calling was clear.

But there was one small problem with the book, I realized. Mary Anna had made a point of telling me that her mother's missal had Latin in it. To be accurate, she'd purred "It's in *Latin*," the same way the teenage roller-coaster workers at Kings Island loved to sneer, "It's for kids *over* forty-two inches tall."

I remembered that Latin was some sort of ancient Bible-times language, from the summer our Vacation Bible School had an Indiana Jones theme. I knew that most people could not understand it, but that Catholics liked it because it was really old, and they thought maybe it could be their secret code with God, because He is old, too.

I hated to admit it, but maybe Mary Anna was on to something with the Latin. Some of the oldest people I knew were

Memaw and Grandy, and they were always talking about how they didn't understand something or other that Meg and I said because it was "too hip, too young" for them. Maybe to Jesus Christ, English was okay, but it was more like some kind of trashy new slang talk compared with the Latin.

For serious prayer, I could not take any chances with a defective missal.

"Daddy," I finally asked, as Momma got up to clear the dinner plates that night. "What is something older and better than Latin?"

Daddy scrunched up his eyebrows at me, leaned back in his seat, and put his hands on his belly in a way that said *what you have asked is highly spiritual and important to me.* I liked how Daddy did this with me. I always paid attention to whom he did and did not do this with during his "Ask the Pastor" sessions at Sunday School.

"Well . . . I don't know if you could say *better,* but as for the *oldest* language there are, of course, ancient Sanskrit texts that—"

"Older," I interrupted. "I mean, what is the very first language God ever spoke? Way, way back in the Book of Genesis."

"Well," Daddy said, rubbing his chin, "way back at the very beginning He only had Himself to talk to, so I guess He didn't have the need to come up with a language to talk to anyone else. And right after that, it was just Him and the animals, so . . ."

Of course!

"Thanks, Daddy!" I interrupted. I nearly toppled my chair, I got up so fast. If I remembered correctly, my little prayer book *was* the perfect missal after all!

Back in my bedroom, I closed the door and let the book

fall open to the center, where a fuzzy lamb scarred with teething marks and orange crayon sat centerfold, like a perfect offering. Printed over his wool was a prayer that went something like:

> *Bow wow wow*
> *How Blessed is Thou!*
> *For the beasts call his name,*
> *The dog, lamb and the fowl . . .*

At least, that was how I read it. And the moment was far too private for me to ask for help sounding it out. I knelt beside my bed and began. And yes, I felt a little silly trying to mimic the donkey brays with a solemn expression on my face, but I held to the mission. *After all,* I thought, *I bet Latin sounds far sillier and more mealymouthed than animal sounds. He will surely understand me before He understands Mary Anna Stinson. In the Lord's sweet name I pray, Baaa.*

And that was how my secret mission went, night after night.

I prayed bedside every night for nearly two weeks before I finally got a response.

We were about halfway through our letters practice in Mrs. Turner's classroom, and I was in need of some kind of a miracle so that I would not fall asleep out of boredom. In the seat next to me, Ariel Hawkins had made a perfectly curved row of *B*'s. I, myself, had made a much shorter row of *B*'s that looked a little like stacked, deflated tires that were melting over the lines. I knew I was supposed to be staying within those wide light blue boundaries, but the giant goony pencil they gave us all to write with had been fighting with my little hands since the day I picked it up.

Not that I would expect Mrs. Turner to understand. The week before, when she handed me another "do-over" writing sheet (on the top of which was drawn such an uninspiring, soul-stomping sad face that anyone who really cared about nurturing children would not *dare* to use it), I reminded her that I was still the best reader in the class by far, and what did it matter anyway that my letters weren't perfect, so long as you could tell what they were supposed to say? Rather than answer me, Mrs. Turner made me sit out in the hall.

But I got no such reprieve from letter-writing on the day the missal struck—that is, until some angelic impulse prompted Mrs. Turner to get up and announce, "Let's take a break for a while and do some phonics instead. Now, who did we leave off with in our last group reading?"

Ariel raised a meek hand next to me and moved around awkwardly in her seat.

It was a good thing she could write out letters so well, I thought, because the poor girl was practically a mute already. She was the only one in class who had actually cried at the man in the giant mouse costume when I had my Chuck E. Cheese's birthday party. Even Meg's little playgroup friends were braver than that.

Mrs. Turner cleared her throat and recited the first line: "It will cost Moe a dime for a Coke!"

She smiled and paused then, and when Ariel didn't repeat the line aloud right away, she made a little stirring motion at the corner of her mouth.

Now, when Ariel *still* didn't read the sentence, after Mrs.

Turner's coaxing, I was not that surprised. It wasn't entirely because of Ariel's shyness, either. *Maybe she's thinking what I'm thinking*, I thought, *that that is a very stupid sentence.* Phonics sentences almost always were. I could not, for the life of me, understand how they were supposed to make us serious about reading when they were full of people with names no one ever heard of, like "Moe" and "Julio," doing things like trying to buy a Coke with just a dime.

Finally, Ariel Hawkins opened her mouth.

But she did not speak. In fact, I cannot tell you exactly what she did, except that at the end of it all, the whole top of her desk was covered with the Tater Tots casserole we'd had for lunch.

For a moment, everyone was silent. We were all looking at Mrs. Turner's face, wondering secretly, I think, if Ariel was going to get in trouble for what she did. It didn't take long for Ariel to break the silence herself, moaning and sobbing while who-knows-what came out of her nose.

Mrs. Turner grabbed a wad of Kleenex tissues from the box on her desk and rushed to Ariel's seat, making *shhh* sounds as she cleaned up the poor child. "Why didn't you tell me you were going to be sick?" she whispered.

Oh, because you always *listen to someone's good reasons for doing something, Mrs. Turner*, I wanted to say.

Mrs. Turner walked Ariel up to the front of the room and sat her in a chair by the teacher's desk. Then she felt her forehead and placed upon it a little strip thermometer (the kind that has a row of light-up colored squares, and that I always imagined could pass for a tiara if you were in the hospital and didn't have any better dress-up clothes, or something).

While our teacher summoned the janitor from the hall, I kept looking at Ariel. There she was, crowned with her thermometer and looking as bedraggled as could be. Almost like she'd been struck with a surprise punch intended for someone else.

And that's when it hit me. When I glimpsed the poster of barnyard animals over Ariel's head, I remembered my missal. I remembered my fervent prayer that my classmates would not have to suffer like this, that I would take on the suffering for them. And the telethons, and the front-page newspaper articles, and anything else Christ needed to bring His people together in a united prayer for healing. And that's when I knew it in my heart—while Ariel Hawkins had been paying worship to proper curves and slants and dotted lines—the affliction meant for me had fallen upon her.

But that couldn't be the whole story. No, Jesus never made mistakes at all, even when it came to making the right people sick. That's what Mrs. Mounts was always saying, anyway. I did not want to be blasphemous by thinking otherwise. What if I did that, and then God heard the thought and got angry and vengeful and gave the whole class the diabetes? Memaw's friends were always getting struck with the diabetes. That was definitely the type of affliction that hit people in droves. One got it, then another got it worse, then another got it with twenty times the aches and pains—

Wait—that was it! It wasn't that Ariel had been hit *instead* of me, I realized. It was that I had probably been hit so hard that part of the affliction had spread over to her, by accident. My body was just a stronger temple, so the symptoms hadn't shown up in me as fast.

After a few minutes, a grainy voice summoned Ariel from within the intercom box on the wall. Mrs. Turner told us to stay in our seats and keep practicing our letters while she walked our poor classmate to meet her mother. And everyone but me obeyed and did just that. I couldn't. No, I stared at those lines on that paper, like jail bars all set to have me sweat behind them for the next half hour, and I knew what I had to do. I said a silent prayer for courage, then I marched straight to the front of the room and sat down in the sick chair by Mrs. Turner's desk.

Suddenly the room got noisy again. The row full of boys by the window (who had to sit there because they didn't behave well to begin with) started a chorus of that sound that is like a hum and a siren mixed together, the one that you used when some other kid was in trouble, and for once, you were not. In the front row, Tabitha Stein snapped that I was "going to get in so much trouble."

I just kept my head up, crossed my ankles, and arranged the folds of my jumper on the seat. After all, certain other people of whom I was aware had also been made to endure taunts and sneers and stones on their journeys of great sacrifice. I could do this. I was *meant* to do this. This was a true test of spirit, and I had to have faith in the affliction I was sure I'd been blessed with, ricocheting off of the strange ark that was pitiful Ariel Hawkins.

Still, I could not help from gulping a bit when I saw Mrs. Turner's wide shadow, lumbering around the door frame ahead of her.

"I thought I said no talk—"

It had taken Mrs. Turner a good second and a half to notice that Ariel had covered her desk with throw up. But the sight of me, sitting in a chair and looking every bit the most polite one in the room, well, that seemed to just about knock her out on the spot.

"Miss Hancock," she said. Then she finished the sentence by snapping her fingers and pointing back toward my desk. I hoped at that moment that the *hmmmmmm* from the row by the window would start up again, just so she could have someone else to get mad at while I fell through a hole in the floor. But no one even made a whimper. The inside collar of my blouse started to feel tight and hot and itchy.

"I . . . ," I began, not wanting to immediately disobey, but not wanting to lessen the impact of my illness by demonstrating that I was still capable of walking.

". . . I . . . I think I am sick, too. Yes, I am sick and you should take my temperature now, please."

My teacher slowly folded her arms. Her glasses were thick like the bottoms of bottles, and that made her eyes tiny and difficult to read. But from what I could tell, it didn't seem like she was angry. The look on her face was more like the kind a grown-up wears when a kid has said a curse word, but the kid heard the word from the adult in the first place. Finally, she just muttered something I couldn't understand at the ceiling and walked behind me to her desk.

She rummaged in the top drawer for a moment, and I felt my bottom tighten up underneath me. Mrs. Turner put another tiara-shaped thermometer on my forehead. And then she bent down on the ground next to me and whispered:

"Now, Miss Hancock, you know I like you very much. But if this temperature comes back normal, you and I are going to have a serious talk about telling tales and looking for attention.

This is not Sunday School. You do not get to be Queen Bee all the time here, young lady."

I tried to nod, but Mrs. Turner said I should sit still and try not to move even a bit.

The next few moments, while Mrs. Turner passed the thermometer time by walking around the room checking papers, I thought about one of my daddy's sermons. He'd talked once about being "imprisoned by doubt," and it left me wondering where a person might find the "doubt prison." Well, now I knew for sure. It was the chair-side desk in the first-grade classroom at Tucker's Mill Elementary.

I had taken weeks to get here, worshipping God and praying to God for a moment of glorious self-sacrifice. But now, I couldn't hear Jesus speaking to me at all. I could only hear a hundred creaking pencils all around me, scribbling out my falsehoods. I knew I didn't really feel sick. I knew I'd lied. And I knew there was only one thing to do.

"Mrs. Turner?" I managed to choke, through a neck that felt guilt-swollen past my shoulders.

"Hold on! Here I come," she said. But before I could get another word out of my mouth, she'd glided to the front of the room and peeled the temperature strip from my forehead.

I finally lifted my head high enough to look at her, and felt the tears start to rise. I waited for the wrath I knew I deserved while she looked back and forth from the temperature strip to me.

"Well I'll be darned," she finally said, putting the back of her wrist to my forehead. "I'll have your mother's classroom paged and we'll see if she can't take you on home. Unless this thing is broken, you're in for a sick, sick day, young lady."

I put my own hand on my forehead, and I nodded.

An hour later, Momma was asking me to please take that hand off my forehead. I hadn't moved it since Mrs. Turner's classroom, and had held it in place past the checkout desk at Tucker's Mill Elementary, all the way through the drugstore checkout line, and all the way home, where Momma struggled to put me into my best pajamas.

I finally obeyed her, but I was hesitant because I wasn't entirely sure what would happen when I moved the hand. Would locusts maybe fly out of my brain? Would prophecies be written over my forehead skin? In Latin?

Dear Lord, what have I done?

I wasn't sure if the chills Momma said I was feeling weren't more out of fright than anything else. I'd offered myself to the Lord to be a vessel for a miracle and it had happened. Actually *happened.* I knew I should have been rejoicing, had I not been so completely terrified.

But is the not-rejoicing a sin, I thought. *Are these the kinds of horrible "doubts" Daddy described?* Just thinking those kinds of heavy things made me dizzy, and I asked Momma if I could lie down. She made me a special nest on the den couch, with a tray and a just-in-case bucket.

As I felt my eyelids shut, I wondered if maybe the miracles in the Bible always seemed so great because they were written from the point of view of someone the miracle did not actually happen to. Maybe for everyone who had to go through them, the great mystery of miracles was that they were horrible. Joy and awe and adoration were just the side effects of realizing it wasn't happening to you.

It didn't seem like much time had passed when I felt

LESSON 6. PATIENCE

Momma shaking my shoulders, hard. But the light was gone from the windows. Even if I hadn't been able to open my eyes—which it almost felt like I couldn't—I would have been able to feel that something heavy and dark was settling over the house. Still, the lights in the room seemed far too bright for what was happening, and sometime in the midst of it all, it felt like someone had wedged two knives into the sides of my neck.

"Momma, stop!" I yelped, grabbing my head to stop the pain from radiating down through my shoulders.

Momma stopped right away and rubbed a damp cloth across my forehead. She sat back on her knees and put her hands together, as if she was praying. I'd seen her do this a hundred times, in the pure, happy way that I supposed all Mommas did it. But something about this was different, awkward. My mother's eyes seemed confused, as if she was completely unpracticed at falling before the Lord in this manner. Almost as if her body had not been made to do this kind of praying at all.

"Thank you, dear Jesus, she's making some sense," she whispered. "Honey, honey, do you know . . . do you remember anything about what you just said? Anything?"

I shook my head. I wanted to tell her that I remembered saying something, but I couldn't. Whatever that affliction was—the thing that had tapped me from up above that morning at school and made my forehead radiate warmth—had scraped its long fingernails down the back of my throat while I slept. And now it was at the bottom of my stomach, stirring, stirring . . .

I sat up too late and barely missed the just-in-case bucket.

195

With my head down, I noticed that my pajama top was covered with stains of other recent "just-missed" moments that I couldn't remember. There were big, still-wet spots around each of them, where someone had done her best with a washcloth.

No wonder Momma was so upset, I thought. She was so excited when I'd opened up those fancy new pajamas on my birthday.

"That's okay, sweetie, that's okay. Just let it all come out," Momma whispered. It was her prayer voice again. She either couldn't or wouldn't shut it off.

"Sharon, here, I've got Geneva Gordon on the phone again," Daddy said, running into the room at a pace that made me almost as uncomfortable as Momma's prayer tone. "She says Joe is up at the hospital tonight."

Daddy squatted and took over Momma's place at the couch while Momma took the phone and paced back and forth by the window. I strained to hear what she was saying, even though she was trying to keep quiet. Her voice was sounding a little bit like old Miss May's singing voice (the oldest soprano in the church choir), I realized. She tried to keep it smooth and on the beat, but every now and then a bad high note would fly out by accident and hit you in the face. These fell mostly at the end of Momma's sentences, and I could hear them from the couch:

"... thought it was just the *flu* ... fever never been this high, *ever* ... four times in an *hour* ... *hallucinating* ... can't move her *neck* ... just staring at the window, talking about bright stars coming to *get her* ..."

Momma hung up the phone and looked over at Daddy. Before she even spoke, he'd wrapped me up in the old blue couch afghan and picked me up like a baby.

"Geneva had Joey paged to the phone. He said we need to bring Emy in to the ER door at Calvary Children's, and we need to get there *now*."

By the time she finished the instruction, Daddy was already halfway to the garage with me. He put me into the backseat, and we pulled into the driveway and sat with the motor running.

If my mind had been clear, and if red blotches hadn't kept forming behind my eyes every time I tried to focus on something, I might have been able to explain to everyone why they shouldn't worry. This was all part of my mission, and soon I'd be healed and everything would be taken care of, after my condition had been fully used to His glory. They just didn't get it, because this was my miracle and not theirs. I would take this one on for them.

But all that came out of my mouth was a moan. And for the moment, I was glad that was all.

"It's okay, baby," Daddy said into the rearview. "We're just going to take a little trip to the hospital and get you feeling better. You remember Miss Geneva's son Joey, don't you? He's a resident there in the children's emergency room. We called him special, and he is specially in charge of you."

I was glad it was dark inside our station wagon, so that Daddy couldn't see that out of everything he and Momma had done to try to make me feel better—all the debris of wasted cold cloths, half-digested aspirin, and undrunk glasses of flat 7UP that I'd seen strewn around the couch when I woke up—the idea that Joe Gordon was waiting for me worked the best of all.

While the girls in my class generally despised boys our own age, we had crushes on all boys who were older. This was especially true when it came to teenage boys. I was in a special and very well-respected position among my female classmates, because my daddy was a pastor of the biggest Baptist church in town, and therefore he was the boss of the biggest Baptist youth group in town. That meant that I got to be acquaintances with more teenage boys than anyone else, because they were always coming over to do young men's Bible study group with Daddy on our deck, or to mow the yard or help nail something or other to the house. Daddy said the only ones who did this were bossed by mommas who were trying to curry favor with the pastor, but you'd have never known it by the way they smiled and took glasses of water from me while they did their hardest yard work. They enjoyed basking in the glow of the pastor's home just as much as anyone, I was sure of it.

And of all those boys who came over, in my mind, none could beat Joe Gordon. He'd gone off to medical school a long time ago, but I could still see him in my dreams, coming up our driveway. He looked a little like Daddy, except for shorter, and he never once said no or that he was too busy when I asked him to look at one of my drawings, or Meg wanted him to see how fast she could ride her Big Wheel down the driveway. He seemed to like the pastor's kids just because he liked them, and not because he was trying to make up for some sin from Homecoming Weekend (this was what Momma always joked about, whenever she saw one of the boys in work clothes coming up the driveway).

After a few minutes, Momma came out the front door dragging my sister, who was stumbling around with half-closed eyes, wearing red rubber rain boots over her footy pajamas. Daddy pointed at the boots as Momma corralled Meg into her car seat, but Momma mumbled something about it being a compromise and said that Daddy should "just go, hurry."

I don't think we passed a single other soul on the way to Calvary Children's Hospital that night. But when we got there, Lord I swear it, you'd have thought the entire world was summoned awake for this one special arrival.

There in Daddy's headlights, a sea of blinding white coats lit up the sidewalk in front of the emergency room entrance.

So this was what it was like to draw people forth into the Lord's power.

Joey Gordon was standing square in the middle, and he looked as handsome as I remembered him. The only problem was, I had pictured him wearing the brightest white coat of all—sort of like the Gabriel of all his doctor friends. But he wasn't wearing a coat, just something that looked a little like an old sweat suit. I decided that was okay.

Everyone crowded around my car door so quickly that it was hard for Daddy to open it more than an inch or two. A little blond nurse, whom I thought I remembered as one of the cheerleaders from the youth group a couple of years ago, nearly scratched the paint on the wagon as she tried to outdo all her other little wheelchair-bearing friends. When the light caught her eyes, she reminded me of a younger version of a church greeter lady.

"Tammy, no," Joe said, stepping into the light and waving her away. "I'll take care of her."

And with a wink so sparkling I could have found it in the dark, Joey Gordon, great physician and former captain of the teenage saved, whisked me from the backseat and carried me inside. Daddy kept pace right next to us and held my hand. I tried to focus my eyes hard on his earlobes, in hopes that this would keep me from throwing up on Joey's shoulder.

But for some reason Daddy's ears seemed to be dripping off his face. Daddy, and the ceiling and floors and everything were melting into a pool at the bottom of my eyelids.

Joey began to walk faster. I could tell that he was speaking to me; I could feel the rumble through his chest and into mine. But I couldn't make out any words. Everything seemed to be slowing while everyone around me was moving faster and faster.

The next hour, the melting got faster still—faces melted into faces and thermometers into Popsicles and hugs from Momma into needles; whirring and blurring and getting hotter.

Until finally, it stopped. I woke up and the world was still again. My skin didn't feel hot anymore, except for my hands, and I could feel the cold of a metal table underneath me. I started to call for someone to do something about the fever in my hands, but then I looked down and saw that Momma and Daddy were holding each of them. They were holding them tight enough to start fires in my little palms.

I wanted badly to talk to them, to tell them that this was all my fault. I'd crossed the line and prayed where I wasn't supposed to. Now look what I had done. Look what I had done to my poor momma and daddy and Joe and everyone else. On the left side of the bed, I could see up close how the cuffs of my momma's jacket were frayed around the edges. She'd wanted a new jacket for a long time. I'd seen her looking at them in the Dawahare's window. But she'd given up having new things so that her little girl could have new coats and new food and be clothed and fed and happy. And this was how I paid her back.

I tried to swallow my tears, because I was afraid they'd hurt my mother more. There was probably a raveling on that frayed jacket cuff for every tear she'd shed on my behalf. I tried to swallow, but the swelling was still crawling over my throat like kudzu, and I could only try to cough out an apology.

As it turned out, it didn't matter anyway because right at that moment Nurse Tammy came bursting through the door, this time wielding a one-eyed teddy bear. She placed it on my bed as if it were the greatest healing balm you could ever imagine. All I could think about when I looked at it, though, was that some good pastor's kid, somewhere, had probably had to give it up because his mother said he had to participate in the children's hospital toy drive or burn in hell. I thought of Petunia, my pet kitty cat of one day, and wondered what suffering child she might be comforting, right then.

"Reverend Hancock!" Tammy beamed, turning to my daddy, "whenever you're done in here, I was just wondering if you could make the rounds, like you did last month? Some of the kids are still awake and I know they'd just looooove ..."

"Not tonight, I'm afraid," Daddy said. There wasn't even a hint of a tear at the edge of his voice. But I knew that didn't mean there weren't any to be shed. They were just locked away at home right now.

"You're right," Tammy went on. I wondered if she got plugged into a life machine at night, like the one my grandmother Mimi was on. Her ponytail vibrated like she might be electrical or something. "Better wait till there's a little more daylight and we have a bigger audience. Oh, I'll never forget that song you did ... did you bring your guitar, by chance? Because I'd be happy to get it for you if it's in the car ..."

Daddy did not have time to reply. The heavy metal door to the room swung open like it was made of nothing, and in walked two people in costume. At least, it seemed like they were in costume at first.

But when one of the characters spoke, I recognized the voice.

"Well, sorry it took us so long." Miss Geneva knocked a hair curler out of her face and rearranged the folds of her jacket so that it better covered her feathered nightgown.

"We love you, little Emy," Miss Ginny purred, adjusting the fur collar of her robe as she slid along my bedrail. Her voice was singsongy as ever, even after midnight.

"And now," she said, turning to my mother and motioning to the corner of the room. "We'll be taking the little one."

"Oh ..." My mother gave Miss Ginny a perplexed look. I craned my neck over the edge of the bed and finally saw what they were talking about—Meg, quickly losing interest in a tattered coloring book over in the corner of the room. I was way beyond surprised that she was not asleep. But no one was themselves this night. Along with making myself sick, I'd managed to make strange creatures out of everyone I knew— Daddy was in a place of the downtrodden but not preaching; Momma was not calm. And my former Sunday School teachers had flown in from the night like strange exotic birds with no makeup on.

"Well," Miss Geneva said, looking over her glasses, just like Momma was a stubborn pupil, "you know, of course, that this hospital is no place for a child who isn't sick. Y'all've got your hands full with the one daughter here, and I've got an empty crib at my house that the grandchildren use. We'll be taking care of Meg for the rest of the night, or however long this takes."

Momma looked too exhausted to argue. She and Miss Geneva helped Meg into her boots while Miss Ginny came over and patted my forehead.

And that was when the epiphany came over me. There, with Miss Ginny looking over me, the too-bright bulb in the ceiling making her look haloed in her hair rollers, something was jolted up and out of my memory. For a moment, I thought I was getting sick again, but I wasn't. It was just the memory—Miss Ginny, in our Sunday School room, talking about the day that old Miss Phoebe died in the church cafeteria. I could hear her words, mixed in somewhere with the hum coming from the hallway—

Sometimes God takes his best angels back to heaven with him!
My heart began to pound against the metal bed.
Oh no. I'd had it wrong all along.

If you worshipped hard and prayed hard, God might use you as an example of an earthly miracle and heal you. But I'd forgotten that if you were *too* good at it—which I had to confess, by my upbringing, I probably was—He might just take you back to heaven to work for Him. Miss Ginny had tried to lay out this path to Baptist sainthood long ago in my kindergarten days, during the hour of Miss Phoebe's death. But woe, I had been too naive and blind to understand it.

I couldn't hold it in anymore. My throat seemed as though it might split open from the pain as I began to cry. I was hurting and I couldn't see, and all at once all the good understandings I thought I'd collected so carefully along my spiritual journey, like patent-leather church shoes lined up neatly in my closet, seemed tarnished and stupid and strange.

Being a good Christian meant the Lord would bless you. But on the other hand, you might just die from all the blessing. It was kind of like taking drugs, the way our school nurse had described taking drugs in assembly. Maybe it was what had happened to Mimi. Maybe it was ordained in our family's blood to happen again.

"Oh, there there there," Miss Ginny said. "What's the matter, darling, you're in wonderful hands! Why my Joe himself . . ."

"You said I would die!" I blurted. The words cracked the roof of my mouth, and I coughed out the rest of the sentence between sobs. "You said God . . . God took . . . the best angels . . . and when Miss Phoebe . . . died . . ."

"Aha, you see!" Miss Geneva came out of nowhere and slapped a rolled magazine against Miss Ginny's arm. I had no idea where she got it, but Miss Geneva always managed to make rolled magazines appear out of nowhere when her sister was around.

"I told you not to tell those kids that business about Phoebe and now look what you've gone and done!"

Miss Ginny took a deep breath and kept smiling. I knew that smile, too. It was her smile from the day at the turkey farm. She bent down low to me, like she had to impart a sacred secret.

"Well, yes, now sometimes that is true. But what many people don't know is, God doesn't take children until they can write their full name on the holy roll, using appropriate penmanship. Isn't that right, Miss Geneva?"

Miss Geneva closed her eyes and nodded solemnly. "Yes. Yes, unfortunately, that is true. Now, when I was helping your mother dress Meggie over there, she was telling me that you told Mrs. Turner that you didn't want to learn to write because you didn't think it was very important. You said God gives some people some gifts and some people other gifts, and it wasn't for Mrs. Turner to question His will, isn't that right?"

I turned my head to the other side of the bed and saw Momma smile for the first time that night.

"You can't write your name, so I'm afraid you're stuck down here with all us angels who aren't good enough yet."

Before she'd finished the sentence, I felt my heart start to slow and my chest cool off. All Daddy's prayers, all Tammy's songs, and all Joey's needles hadn't been able to do that the whole night. I wondered why, with all the great learned spiritual men in the world, with TV pulpits and robes of purple velvet, no one ever made as much sense as the old church ladies. Nobody. It was always the ones who were almost frail enough to see through that made you feel the most solid about the Lord.

As the Misses G and G were leaving, with Meg dragging behind and searching one of their purses for breath mints, Joey came back into the room.

"Reverend, could I speak to you just a moment? We're going to be doing one more procedure."

Daddy and Joey went over to the corner of the room, which was only a couple of feet or so from the edge of my bed. Joey was wearing his most serious expression of the night, and I pointed out to Momma that this was funny because painted on the wall behind his head was a drawing of a cross-eyed elephant with the measles. Momma shushed me. She wanted to eavesdrop, so we did it together. It wasn't hard, though. Neither the doctor nor the preacher was very good at speaking quietly.

"... spinal meningitis ... just a precaution, only way to rule it out ... there has been a case reported, two counties away ..."

Daddy nodded and winked at me. "Nothing our earth angel can't handle, is it? One more needle, kid?"

I tried to smile. I'd save the tears for this needle for my own burden box. My momma didn't look like she could handle any more from me.

Joey left the room, and came back a second later followed by Tammy and two other men in doctor's sweat suits that were green instead of blue. Both were carrying what looked like small seat belts, and they both pulled me up, a little too fast, and moved me to the edge of the bed.

Then I saw a look of fear in my daddy's eyes that I hadn't seen, ever.

"Wait, wait," he said, his voice panicked. "What are you doing?"

"Oh, those are just the restraints," Joey said. He was moving around some items on a tray. The top of the tray was covered with a paper towel, patterned with a bright clown holding balloons. As he jostled the tray, the towel slipped. What I saw peeping out from under it looked more like a long-bit drill than a needle.

I started to wriggle away from the men. Daddy would understand why I had to take back my promise to endure one more needle, because this *was not a needle*.

"No, she's frightened," Daddy said. Joey still wasn't looking up. "Is that necessary? She's a good girl, she'll be still if you tell her to—"

"I'm afraid we can't risk it," Joey said. "We're going into her spine, and there could be serious complications if she moves, even a little bit. I'm sorry, I know how you feel but we have to do it."

"Fine then," Daddy said. "No restraints. I'll hold my little girl."

"But, Reverend, our policy—"

"I said I'll hold my daughter."

Joey stared Daddy in the eye for a second, then turned away, mumbling something about how Daddy would have to sign a release. Suddenly, I felt strong enough to elbow both the sweat-suit men out of the way at the same time (though of course, I did not). I had never seen Daddy give an order to a church congregant like that, without the pulpit and the fear of God between the two of them. And it had actually worked.

Daddy sat on the edge of the bed and moved me onto his lap. Then he turned me crossways across the front of him, so that my head was over his shoulder.

Momma stood behind us and held on to both my hands, and I couldn't tell which one of the three of us was shaking the hardest.

Everything in the room was silent. Tammy didn't make a sound as she wiped the alcohol over the bottom of my bare back, and I think the chill must have come through my bones and hit Daddy, because I thought I heard him make a shivering sound.

Then I realized, he wasn't shivering. He was humming. It was some sort of a hymn, I thought at first. But it couldn't be, it didn't have all the glory and rumbling about it that a hymn has. And then he added the words, so slowly and softly that even the doctors couldn't hear them. And I remembered.

. . . don't you ever ask them why . . . if they told you you would cry . . . just look at them and sigh . . . and know they love you.

Somehow, in the midst of holding me, under the clang of metal against metal and the high-pitched harmonic of worry rising under the fluorescent lights, Daddy had conjured something to hold him. It was a peace that rested in the old testament of his memory, and it resurrected itself with a melody that passed through all generations, big enough and long enough to shoulder the burdens he could not endure alone, and rhythmic enough to make sense of them.

And slowly, slowly, even though I knew Daddy was holding me still with all his might, I could swear I felt his shoulders and face and heart relax. All the pipe organs were miles away, far beyond thick metal doors. I knew that I wouldn't stand to sing a hymn in church again without looking up in the choir loft and imagining Crosby, Stills, Nash, and Young, sitting there in robes, relaxed and willing to be soothers and healers, unlikely gods and guides for whomever needed them. And I'd look around at the faces of my father's friends in the congregation—the ones he knew from college and seminary; the ones I knew, from pictures, had once had long hair and mustaches, too—and I'd wonder if they weren't seeing the same thing.

When the sky was barely daylight, Miss Ginny, who proclaimed that Momma and Daddy would be far too tired to drive, picked us up from the Calvary Children's Hospital.

"Joe said it was the most severe reaction to the strep virus he's ever seen in a child," Ginny said, putting on her lipstick in the rearview. "You should call Carol Turner and tell her right away. Someone in her classroom is probably a carrier."

My mother nodded. Yes, she would surely tell Mrs. Turner the truth—pure viral evil was transmitted by a row of perfectly written *B*'s.

I sat in the back and clutched my prescription bag, and the one-eyed teddy that had somehow miraculously found its way from donor preacher's kid to donee preacher's kid. I supposed it was only right. When it came to the heavy task of being God's earth angels, we had it worse than most.

Daddy held me one more time that morning before he tucked me into bed. Before he left my room, I took the missal out from under my pillow and handed it to him. I told him to take it and to lock it up somewhere, where Meg couldn't find it. Where no child could ever get ahold of it again.

Lesson 7

Aunt Kit and Momma at an Acteen coronation service

Joy

QUEENS OF THE HOLY WILDERNESS

Inside nearly every Southern Baptist Church in America, you will find five standard pieces of furniture: the organ, the altar, the pew, the pulpit, and the trophy case. This last item in the list, perhaps the most puzzling to outsiders, is also the most important. And no, it is not actually a shrine, or an urn case, or any other such ghastly thing full of blood and bones. It is just as it seems, and it holds the most sacred objects of the church's mission: awe-inspiring softball trophies, revered by the holy and unholy in the community alike; donated Bibles that are too fancy to read; a gold-plated groundbreaking shovel that is taking up too much space (but that you don't dare move because it would offend the sensibilities of Miss Such and Such's grandmother, whose daddy donated that shovel, and without whom the church would not exist, period).

When I was twelve years old, the trophy case at Hart's Creek Baptist, down the road from where we'd moved when my father took a job at the Kentucky Baptist Convention, held one jewel in particular, a thing so pure, so golden and light-filled, that I was sure its beams had been drawing me to it, even as my family cut a crooked path of ministry across the Bluegrass: the Acteen Queen tiara.

I longed for that crown so deeply in my soul that my belly

burned when I drew near it. And partly because of the reverence I held for it, I tried to keep my gazing sessions with that beautiful crown private. I was beginning to understand that if you wanted something bad enough, you had to go off and pray about it all by yourself (not just wait for the Sunday-morning crowd to tell you that it was an okay thing to pray for, and then join in with you). My father himself had said from the Hart's Creek pulpit, when he was guest preacher, that the best Christians were Christians when nobody was watching, and who did not act for man's glory alone.

But I knew—and the good, selfless Christians at Hart's Creek must have understood, too—that the Acteen tiara far outshown the glory of man. It was the sort of rhinestone-and-electroplated perfection whose creation *just had* to be divinely inspired.

There was a second reason why I never let anyone see me gawking at the crown. Normally, in every other church I had been so blessed to grace, I'd felt bulletproof. I'd marched inside the vestibule right in time with the white vibration of my father's sermons, and had never had the thought of a misstep. No one else, blinded by my family's royal radiance, had ever dreamed that I'd be less than sparkling patent leather, over insides starched with goodness. They were told so in the Sunday-morning program, and in the church bulletin after that—"Reverend Hancock, award-winning preacher of the Lord, is married with two young daughters. We trust that the other mothers and children of this church will show them a warm welcome, or be sacrificed and served at the hayride." Or something like that. At least, they mostly behaved toward us as if that was the instruction they'd been given.

But Hart's Creek was different. It was the first church I'd ever been a full-time member of where Dr. Jeremiah Ford, *not* my father, was the pastor. Not that we should feel strangely about that, Momma said. It was, after all, a "big step up" for Daddy. With a Convention post, he might not be preaching from a pulpit every Sunday, but he got to do it from behind a desk every other day of the week. Whenever she said this, I always pictured Daddy in one of those big computer control rooms, like on *Star Trek*, watching live sermons on hundreds of screens and pushing a laser-zap button whenever some poor pastor said a Beatitude wrong, or elected a deacon who'd been divorced twice, or forgot to smile.

I wasn't sure, though, if the congregants at Hart's Creek really appreciated this power. For all they knew, the Reverend Hancock was just the fill-in host on the Sundays when Dr. Ford was on vacation, and the guy who cut the ribbon on the new Christian Rec Center; a strange sort of dignitary, one who you were supposed to know was famous, but really didn't.

And when it came to my chances for future missions awards, sad as it was, their ignorance worried me. Sure, Acteens was just the missions achievement program after GAs, the one everyone went into when she turned thirteen (even if you were a complete Bible-illiterate and only forced to come to church because you'd been caught tongue-kissing a boy or something by your single chain-smoking momma, who suddenly decided church was a good idea. I kept mentioning to my father that the Acteens really ought to be more selective). And the crown was the prize that signified you'd completed the important, the infamously treacherous first level in the

Acteen program. Whereas GAs had been nothing more than making up rhymes about kindness, Acteens meant essays about the church stewardship program, to be read and evaluated by the trustees; where GAs was woolly tights, macaroni crafts, and presentations to grateful mommas, Acteens was pantyhose, casserole baking, and quiet coffee service at Brotherhood meetings. Plus, there was the big project, a single-handed missions endeavor you had to design and complete in order to secure a place and a crown at the coronation ceremony.

It was this last part that put a knot in my stomach every time I passed the trophy case—a faithlessness in my piety that I didn't want anyone to witness as it crept onto my cheekbones. 'Cause everywhere I'd been, I could see that making the Queen level was as much about making connections as it was about making pot holders for the homeless. The Acteen director always had final say as to whether or not your project was "appropriate" (teen pray-a-thon for missions, yes; teen dance-a-thon for missions, no). More than that, she controlled who, from the church's list of more elite members, got called in to assist you. I had once heard of an Acteen, who was fortunate enough to be the daughter of a Women's Missionary Union president, overseeing the sewing of a hundred jumpers for the naked tribeswomen of Djibouti—"assistance" courtesy of a member who owned a local sewing machine shop and greatly appreciated the patronage of the WMU members over the years.

It wasn't a bad system, in my opinion. Being Baptist was clearly getting so popular, thanks to the efforts of people like my father, that there simply wasn't room for all the people who wanted to do top missions work. Potentially subpar toy

drives had to be quashed before they took up valuable time
and limited offering money. Someone had to do the cutting;
someone had to make the decisions. Someone had to respect
a system where you fought with all your soul to wear a crown.
After all, Jesus had, now, hadn't He?

At all our other churches, my mother might have wielded
that kind of influence as pastor's wife. But walking the hallways
of this new church, she was more like Queen Elizabeth on a
visit to the United States. She was revered as a Conventioneer's
wife, of course, but she wasn't really allowed to be the boss of
anyone. Not under the Hart's Creek steeple. If I wanted to
make the kind of connections that would get me to that coronation stage, I was going to have to do them on my own. And
I was going to have to start early, too, though it was a full year
before I'd even be eligible to attend my first Acteens meeting.

By the grace of God, my perfect opportunity came on
the Sunday before my twelfth birthday. I was nearing the end
of what had seemed like an absolutely eternal service, made
longer by the fact that I'd worn an early birthday gift from
Momma: my first pair of church-girl heels. They were white
(smooth and lady-like, not shiny and cartoony like the patent
Mary Janes I'd worn the week before). Technically, I knew
they only qualified as "high heels" in the way that Louisville,
Kentucky, was the "big city." They were only slightly elevated
above the flat ground all around them. But (just ask any Louis-
villian you ever meet) this was enough.

In my mind, that three-quarters of an inch of wood underneath my heels brought me that much closer to the front
balcony, the one that was especially large and grand at Hart's
Creek, but that I'd seen, in some shape or form, in every

Baptist church I'd ever been in. This was where the teen and teenish girls sat (those from the Marys and Marthas Sunday School group; the Deborah's Followers; even a few from the Salt and Light college coed group) in a neat row, hands deftly passing lip glosses and Sunday School notes between purses with matching Bible covers, legs crossed neatly in a line under *straight* tweed skirts—no hint whatsoever of ruffles that flounced when they walked, like wild baby bird feathers, or sleeves puffed up so big it looked like their mothers had tried to inflate them toward heaven.

But after one morning in those heels, it made me wonder how the balcony girls managed to keep their happy, giggling expressions all service long. I'd already had to skip out of Sunday School to ask Momma for a pair of Band-Aids to spare my ankles. (This didn't bother me, of course, because it only served to draw everyone's attention to the fact that I was, in fact, wearing heels, and more important, that Katrina Clare's wearing of her training bra to choir practice the week before had just been a big waste of time on her part, because we all had to put on robes. And Katrina hardly had anything that could be noticed from the choir loft, anyway.)

I managed to keep my feet stuffed inside my pumps all the way through the benediction and was almost ready to skip toward the vestibule when Dr. Ford made the announcement. All girls in the upper GA levels were invited to stay for a few moments after service, when Lois Bullman would be distributing materials about GA Mother–Daughter Overnight Camp, to be held in beautiful Redemption Gap, Kentucky.

I decided bloody heels were a small sacrifice.

Momma kept looking sideways at me for the next half

hour as my knee bobbed up and down under her glossy brochure of Redemption Gap. The mother and daughter on the front had long hair past their rear ends, and were both playing the guitar and wearing big old baggy sweaters and skirts, even though it was supposed to be a summer camp. But none of this mattered to me. I knew that the GA Mother–Daughter Overnight—the true "capstone to the GA experience," Lois Bullman called it, grasping her own brochure to her chest and sounding as if she might burst into tears—was as important a step in the path to Baptist Womanhood as baptism itself. It was once a year, once in a soul's lifetime, for young ladies of the proper age and path. My own momma had pictures in a scrapbook of her and her sister, Kit, standing creekside at their own GA camp, right next to snapshots of them the following fall, posing as regally as pageant winners in their Acteen crowns.

Even if I hadn't been hearing about the virtues of the magical weekend in Redemption Gap since birth, Lois Bullman would have put the longing for nature right into me. Flashing grainy slides of girls in various stages of summer sweat, she spoke of an "unmatched chance for *growth*," an unforgettable, unmatchable "chance to *become*, to *bloom*, to *develop* in Christ." By the time she was finished, I know half of us preteens in the crowd wondered if skipping the camp meant that God would never let us grow breasts. It was no wonder Lois was rumored to be a top choice for the next year's Acteens leader.

"Bible stuff aside, it really is just a whole lot of fun," Momma said as Daddy drove us to the Hart's Creek parking lot two months later. It was 5 a.m. on the first day of camp, and I had been going on pure excitement and sneaked sips of

Ale-8–One for almost twenty-four hours. I'd tried to sleep, but every time I closed my eyes, the glow of that tiara—*so close*—had pushed my lids right back open again. Lois Bull-man was in for the most inspiring GA overnight she'd ever had in her life, and she didn't even know it. Why, right then, she couldn't even fathom the concept of blessings, volunteered by me in the mess hall when others were too shy to come forward, that would fill mommas and girls so full-up with thankfulness that they couldn't even eat afterward. If someone had told her that an individual existed who was capable of working such awe-inspiring handcrafts in pinecones and glue that an already baptized camp full of girls would take to the waters again, she'd have called them blasphemous.

But Mrs. Lois Bullman was about to be baptized herself. Into the world of a new woman in her wilderness—a kind, quiet soul who had come wandering into her midst one day, surrounded only by rumors that her father was a famous prophet. Yes, Lois Bullman was about to have an epiphany.

". . . and, let's see, they taught us to fish," Momma went on, "and Aunt Kit, well, she of course nearly lost her bathing suit skiing behind the motorboat . . . But hey, the most important part of it all is, you and me will get to spend some good time together. Isn't that right, Em?"

I nodded, still on fire from planning Mrs. Bullman's epiphany. I did feel a little guilty about not being more excited about "bonding" with Momma, but she and I had a lifetime for that sort of stuff. She would understand. The Lord Jesus only managed to corner Paul on the road to Damascus one precious time.

We pulled up behind the church van, where Mrs. Bullman

was stretching her leg against the bumper, like she was preparing for an Everest hike or something. Even though she'd insisted that "no strenuous activity" was involved in this "Christlike wilderness experience." Then again, I thought, she'd also raved and raved, no less than a month ago, about the fantastic superchurch they were building down in Tennessee—about how it was the size of a city block and had a similar skyline, with solid brass fixtures in the sanctuary and rolling electronic message boards instead of hymnals, and obviously no touch of wilderness anywhere. I knew that if I was really going to gain this woman's respect, I was going to have to get on her good side and figure out what she *really* thought glorified God the most. Was it tree bark, or was it solid brass electroplate?

Daddy kissed Momma and me on our foreheads, then flashed the smile that everyone found easily in the dark. The three pairs of mommas and daughters who were traveling with us said hello and gave little giggles. Mrs. Bullman saluted like an army officer.

"Now, you girls be good and learn lots," he said, then led everyone in a circle prayer at Mrs. Bullman's request. Parking-lot circle prayers were a tradition I'd become familiar with long before Hart's Creek. They were bestowed before every Baptist adventure-style activity I'd ever seen—missions trips, choir tours, distribution of tract-stuffed turkeys out in the ghetto. I don't know who started the circles, but I always felt they were sort of like a Christian auto insurance policy. And this was a good thing, given that most church vans had been reincarnated at least twice from former existences as school buses and catering vehicles.

Momma gave Daddy one last hug, and I saw him reach into his wallet and hand her a crisp ten-dollar bill.

"But we won't need any money—"

Daddy just winked and waved her off. I felt a little surge of excitement as Momma folded the money into her billfold. My father didn't just hand out money like that, and the fact that he did this time made me think that he wanted this weekend to be really special. Momma and I were going away unwashed peasants of the suburbs. We were going to return as his Queens of the Holy Wilderness.

Now, though it pains me, I can't exactly say that every daughter in our traveling group was exactly Acteen Queen material. There was Mandy Burnside, who was nice and whose momma sometimes taught our Sunday School class (but read directly from the workbook and didn't offer a single anecdote from her own journey away from sin). But then there was Betsy Reynolds, who was also nice, if a little braggerty, though her momma more than made up the difference. She regularly invited Meg and me over after church to swim in their pool that was shaped like the letter *R*, and when everyone got too tired of that (or, usually, when Betsy got too tired of that), we got to go inside and play in all Mrs. Reynolds's makeup and evening gowns. Mrs. Reynolds sometimes stood out on the rear deck and smoked a cigarette while we were there. She always whispered to me, "Don't tell your momma and daddy, okay?" I appreciated that she realized I could be trusted with a grown-up secret.

But finally, there was Hannah Bullman, Mrs. Bullman's daughter. Hannah was one of those kids who was only okay to a point. And the problem was, you got no advance warning of when that point was. Every time a group of us got together to play, Hannah wound up crying and yelling "I hate you" and moping in the corner by the end, and you were supposed to just guess why she was upset. Mrs. Bullman would come out running to her and fold her up in her arms, like she was a kidnapped child making a homecoming. Then she'd line us all up and say, "I think I know exactly what happened here," and we'd have to say we were sorry to Hannah one by one, even though we didn't know what for.

Mrs. Bullman propped herself up on the back bumper to address all of us. She was wearing a polo shirt that had GA MOTHER-DAUGHTER OVERNIGHT '83 embroidered on the front and was lopsided from the weight of five or six other MOTHER–DAUGHTER OVERNIGHT pins from different years. A veritable major general of the Baptist Momma Corps, she was a force of maternal goodness to be feared.

I could only imagine how many times I was going to end up having to apologize to Hannah Bullman before our road trip was done.

"Good early morning, everyone!" she began, clapping her hands. Everyone snapped to but Hannah, who had her head laid over on her hand and was making mock snoring noises.

"It really and truly thrills my soul to be going on this journey with each and every one of you. I'd like to extend a special welcome to Sharon and Emy Hancock, who are about to embark on their very first Redemption Gap experience."

Mrs. Bullman started clapping really obvious-like, and everyone joined in for a couple of drowsy claps.

"Emy and Sharon," she went on, "I am sure everyone here will tell what an important . . . what an awakening experience this will be for you. Out there, in the middle of His country, with His creations. You truly get a sense for how the earthly mother–daughter bond is but . . ."

Mrs. Bullman gestured in the air, and somewhere to my right, I thought I heard Betsy's momma choke on her tall mug of coffee.

"... how the mother–daughter bond is but a mirror of Christ's love for all His children."

I suddenly had a picture in my mind of Jesus Christ, running through our backyard with curlers in His hair and beard, chasing Meg with a flyswatter and shouting, "Don't you give me that look!"

Before giving us permission to get into the van, Mrs. Bullman said she had to go over a couple of ground rules that had been abused by campers in the past. First, there could be no calls to men, including husbands. In the event of an emergency, a *supervised* phone call could be made from the camp office. (At this, I thought I heard Momma choke on her coffee, along with Mrs. Reynolds. Then I realized she didn't have any coffee.) Trousers were not permitted to be worn in the camp chapel, though nice culottes were acceptable. (Momma leaned down and whispered the explanation she knew I'd need, that culottes were something she'd worn when she was a little girl, about twenty years ago. They looked like baggy old-lady shorts.)

And finally, she said to put our thinking caps on for what we might do for the group skit, the second night of camp. This year's theme was Christian Creativity, with an emphasis on individual gifts and the blessings of self-expression. She also said that makeup of any kind on young ladies under fifteen would be cause for immediate ejection from the camp.

"What, no stoning?" Mrs. Reynolds said, elbowing my momma.

As it turned out, the drive wasn't bad at all. Hannah slept most of the way, whining only when Mrs. Bullman drove through one of the fifty thousand potholes that marked the way down the private road to "one of Baptist America's proudest assets."

I laid my head in Momma's lap, and she played with my hair while I tried to nap. It was nice, just being able to lie back and let my hair go all wild at a church function. Though I loved the robes and starched slips that had taught me good posture over the past eleven years, part of me wished that all church functions could be like this. Just you and your momma, thankful and joyful and praying. No Daddy to come in all the time and pound his fist on the pulpit and interrupt you, even if you needed it once in a while.

FEARSOME MINISTRATIONS

We approached Redemption Gap just as it was getting daylight outside. Mrs. Bullman stopped at a gas station to fill up, and to get a bottle of fruit juice for Hannah, who was *haaaaaaawwwwt*.

When they went inside, Momma and I walked and stretched with Betsy and her momma.

"So tell me the truth," Mrs. Reynolds whispered to Momma. "How are you planning on making it through Frigid Army boot camp?"

Momma just laughed and started to say something that had to do with needing a survival supply of prayer, but Betsy was jumping up and down, shrieking through the trees.

"Look, look! It's even better than ours!"

We all peeked through the elms to what Betsy was pointing at: the greatest-looking swimming pool I had seen in my life, L-shaped and topped off with what looked like a small waterslide. Betsy and I both started jumping up and down. Maybe our wilderness baptism wasn't going to be as rough-and-tumble as Mrs. Bullman made it sound.

"Ah, you found High Mount's pool, I see. Isn't it a beauty?"

It was Mrs. Bullman, behind us.

"High Mount?" Betsy asked.

225

"The RA camp. Boys only," Mrs. Bullman said. "They just redid the pool. Got a new volleyball court, too, and air-conditioning in some of the cabins."

"Air-conditioning!" Mrs. Reynolds shouted. She reached into her purse, where I caught a glimpse of a cigarette pack, but seemed to think better of it and drew her hand back. "Now, I know Redemption Gap doesn't have anything like that, unless they've remodeled the place since last month's brochure."

"Well, n-no," Mrs. Bullman stammered. "No they haven't. We have to remember that that decision was probably made with respect to women's wishes, our wishes. GAs like to think of others first, ourselves last, isn't that right?"

Mrs. Bullman gave us all a pleading sort of look. Her lapel pins had started to sag dangerously close to the ground, exposing a bra strap and making the GA letters on the front look like they were melting.

"Right!" Momma piped up. "Us girls don't need stupid air-conditioning to have fun, do we? Real wilderness queens don't need that!"

Mrs. Bullman looked a little revived. I felt my heart jump a little when she mouthed *thank you* to Momma as we once again climbed in and adhered our legs to the van seats.

Despite Mrs. Bullman's early wake-up call, it looked like we were the last to arrive at Redemption Gap. A long line, made up of clusters of pigtails and matching-colored polo shirts, snaked out of the basement of the rickety chapel, which looked like it had been stuck into a mountainside on toothpicks. Betsy and I stood in front of the van and crossed our arms.

"Nobody told us we were supposed to dress alike," Betsy mumbled. A group of eight or so girls crossed in front of us, wearing khaki shorts with identical pink cardigans. The one who passed nearest to me had KELLY stitched on her front pocket, and CRESTVIEW GA in neat script across her back. She waved graciously and they all waved graciously, like a flock of winged Miss America contestants. Like last year's Championship Cheerleading Squad of Redemption Gap, ponytails bouncing in unison beneath matching bows hand-painted with GOD HEARTS YOU.

I folded my arms tighter in front of me, hoping to smother the humiliatingly glittered unicorn on what used to be my favorite T-shirt. "Kelly" was probably my age, but she looked like she could already walk right into the front row of the balcony—do not pass Go, do not give Deacon Tom a low five.

"Oh, you don't have to. Dress alike, I mean," Hannah said. "A lot of people do, but Mom says it takes away from the experience."

Great, I thought, all because of plain Mrs. Bullman's "experience," I now knew what Redemption Gap must have felt like—flat-chested and pitiful in the glorious, renovated shadow of High Mount.

Maybe that was going to be the lesson of the weekend. That God made woman, and Southern Baptist man made Southern Baptist woman, because it is impossible to be the most glorious unless there's someone around who is more pathetic than you.

We finally made our way into the basement registration room, and Mrs. Bullman jumped to the front of the group again.

"Now," she said, swooping an arm down in front of us like a zoo tour guide who was worried our very presence might threaten some rare, precious species of cockatoo in the room. "These girls you see, lined up behind the registration tables. They will be your leaders, your role models for the next couple of days. Be sure to follow closely and soak up every bit of their influence you can. Because *they* are selected from the top Acteens *in the entire state.*"

Mrs. Bullman made little karate-chop motions with her right hand as she proclaimed those last five syllables. Betsy and I strained up on our toes, craving binoculars that would take our eyes over the big bangs of the East Bethel group, through the precarious space between the Harlan County and Jericho Road groups, where dueling, increasingly vicious versions of "Joy, Joy, Joy, Joy Down in My Heart" threatened to snipe off the heads of passersby.

And then I saw them. Crested and strange as all get-out.

Before I knew it, my heart had already cried out into the wilderness in a plea for forgiveness—because try and pray as I might, I couldn't picture *any* of these girls with crowns on their heads. All of them had legs so pale that, had Mrs. Bullman not pointed them out, they might have disappeared into the wall. Knobby, mosquito-marked knees clanged around inside big old white shorts, so heavy and thick that they looked hotter than any pair of winter pants I owned. Pale pink counselor shirts, shoulder seams almost reaching the counselors' elbows, completed what my art teacher would have called "the pastel wash"—from petal to pale to pallid to dead. Or was it supposed to be, not dead, but angelic? It seemed that when it came to the beauty of the best Christian teenagers, the line was meant to be fuzzy.

As we got closer to the "A through H" check-in table, I realized that considerably more effort had been made by the counselors above the neck (as if gentlemen were invited to that region only). Mada-lynn, the Acteen who welcomed Momma and me forward with one great, gracious swoop of her friendship bracelet and lanyard-strewn forearm, wore purple eyeliner that crept out of line here and there. She popped her retainer in and out of her teeth with her tongue while her sideways ponytail (which my cousin Suzanne had told me was "out" two summers ago) so matted and sprayed with glitter that it had become like a solid wall, twittered back and forth in careful review.

I felt Momma take the back of my elbow. It was a subtle, whispered grip that said, *Now, don't you dare.*

She didn't need to worry, though. I was too stunned to point out anything unusual in the crude faces-of-many-colors, whom we could only hope drew trail maps better than they drew on eyeliner.

Truth be told, I felt more let down than anything. I had always felt nothing but the purest awe for any teenage girl who was allowed to wear cosmetics. It was a good, uplifting kind of awe—jealous, but okay because you knew it was short-lived, you were just a few years away from attaining it yourself.

But I felt sorry for the Acteen counselors, and I felt stupid for myself. *What exactly did you expect an eighteen-year-old girl who has nothing to do with her Friday nights except sew jumpers for the naked tribeswomen of Djibouti to look like?*

It was as if those coroneted Queens of the Holy Wilderness, the ones whose light I'd come this far to bask in, were more like creatures abandoned by the helping hands of real mommas. They'd come out here to follow the Lord, forgetting that He was a boy, and they did not know a darn thing about wooing men with eye shadow. And then one day, an old Avon catalog had drifted down the creek to Redemption Gap. And the Acteens had fished it out, and they'd made a genuine Laura Ingalls effort out of constructing cosmetics of tree bark and craft glitter and prayers.

"Ummm, ma'am?" Mada-lynn said. The bright pink, blushered V that went from her nostrils to her hairline on either side seemed to have reddened a little bit.

"Oh, yes?"

I could tell from Momma's tone that she was trying to pretend that her mind had wandered. That the makeup jobs on Mada-lynn and her co-workers hadn't rooted her eyes to the spot like a car accident.

Mada-lynn looked both ways and leaned across the table.

"Does yer daughter know 'bout the Ministration?"

I couldn't stop the edge of my mouth from turning down at Mada-lynn a little. She could have asked me the question, since I was standing right there. And I would have been glad to answer, had I had any idea what she'd asked.

"I . . . what, could you repeat that?"

Mada-lynn obliged, near a whisper this time.

"Oh, the administration?" Momma finally exhaled. "Well, yes, her father works in the Convention, so Emy could probably tell you the whole structure of the WMU, and the GA board, and . . . is this for a game? One of the camp contests?"

"No," Mada-lynn said. This time, she stood up and got as close to Momma's ear as she could, without crossing over the sacred table.

"I mean, ma'am . . . you fergot to fill out this here part on yer camp form. It asks does yer daughter know 'bout the Ministration."

Momma took back the pink paper to look at whatever Mada-lynn's press-on nail was gesturing toward. To look at her face as she read the line aloud, you'd have thought the suns drawn in the border had singed her fingers:

"Does your camper know about *menstruation*."

Betsy's cupped hand slammed into my ear. I knew what she was going to tell me before it got out of her mouth— "You'll never guess what that counselor girl is talking about to my *mom!*"

"Well, yes she does . . . ," my mother said, her eyes now too tired to dare looking up from the form again. The form was safe. One's thoughts couldn't sin against Eve by just looking at the form.

". . . but what does that have to do with anything?"

Mada-lynn started nodding before Momma finished speaking, and let loose with a speech that sounded like she'd been repeating it all day.

"We've had some ince-dinces in the past, ma'am. In some of our activities, mother daughter are sep'rated. Sometimes, strenuous activities in girls of this age are prone to set off the Ministration. We need to know if they know what it is, if you aren't right there when it happens. And you have to check on the form whether we're allowed tell your girl what's happening or not."

"Well for heaven's sake!" I heard Betsy's momma shout from the next table. "What's the alternative? I mean, if she didn't know, and I said you weren't allowed to tell her, what were you planning on saying if it happened? 'Well, I guess you're dying'? The Great Flood hath arrived? Now the sharks will come?"

My own momma just checked and initialed the form without saying another word.

A woman in the corner of the room who had stringy, short hair plastered to her head and big glasses started squawking through a rusty microphone that everyone should sit down and pay attention. She was Mary Jane Armbruster—our "fearless leader," she squawked, drawing the suck-up laughter of the East Bethel group. *If Mary Jane Armbruster has a crown at home, it probably misses her skinny head entirely and hangs around her neck*, I thought.

"Before we commence with our opening prayer on this very blessed opening day of our overnight, I have a quick moment of devotion to share," she said. "Now, as students of women's missions, we all know that we are witnesses not just with our mouths, but with our actions, *riiiiight?*"

Everyone head-bobbed a yes. Someone in the back, clearly itching for a tiara even more than I was, even let loose with a cheerleaderish "A-men!"

"And what we do is a witness, who we make company with is a witness, even the clothes we wear can spread the word, *riiiight?*"

Three people joined in the Amens.

"Right!" Mary Jane shouted, thrusting a fist in the air. The armholes on her counselor shirt were so big that you could see her bra. It was big and white, like a grandma bra. She had on what must have been the required white shorts, too, but hers were worn way up high on her waist, so that you could almost make out the outline of her popo.

Betsy's mom elbowed Momma. "How many commandments you reckon she's breaking with those shorts?"

Momma tried to keep her pastor's-wife face but snickered in spite of herself.

"Looks like they're breakin' something else, too," Mrs. Reynolds added.

"Oh hush," Momma laughed. "You're going to get us in trouble with the principal."

I smiled. Most kids would assume that the preacher's wife wasn't allowed to take part in conversations about dirty stuff. They thought that, upon hearing one word of what had come out of Betsy's momma's mouth, my mother would faint and disintegrate, just collapse into a pile of the purest white sugar and drift away on the wind. But people like Betsy's momma seemed to have figured out that this wasn't true. They treated Momma like a spiritual representative of course, like the right arm of my daddy, but without the license to persecute. A priest without the vow, she could hear confessions, but she couldn't dole out penance the way Daddy could. That way, she was the ideal "minister" to women like Mrs. Reynolds. Afternoons after WMU, spent chatting and laughing in hushed voices around Bunco cards and pans of chocolate éclair cake, those were the sanctuaries where Momma's followers flocked.

"So, in the spirit of missions-mindedness," Mary Jane went on, "let me unveil this year's official matching mother–daughter apparel! T-shirts are only seven dollars and fifty cents apiece! Please line up in an orderly fashion!"

Hannah, Betsy, and Mandy raced to the front, dragging their mothers by the arms. I felt a deep sense of relief that we weren't going to be the pitiful mismatched group anymore. But then I saw Momma reach into her pocket. She pulled out nothing but the crisp ten-dollar bill Daddy had handed her that morning, and her face fell.

"I'm not getting one if you don't," I said.

"Oh, don't be silly. I have plenty of T-shirts. Go ahead, that's why we have the money in the first place."

I walked with my head down to the line, where Betsy and her mother had already produced plastic tortoiseshell clips from their luggage and were threading the edges of their new T-shirts through them. Hannah and Mrs. Bullman had opted to tuck theirs in, almost to their ankles, it seemed.

"Doesn't your mother want to wear a shirt, like the rest of us?" Betsy asked. I mumbled some lie about Momma being allergic to the fabric. I said it would aggravate her asthma if it wasn't prewashed, and everyone nodded reverently.

I heard a "look over here" and saw Momma looking at me from her place far outside the T-shirt line, through the point-and-click camera she'd borrowed for the trip.

And I felt like the most unworthy Queen there ever was.

After that all-important shopping devotional, Mary Jane told us that the first order of every day would be private mother–daughter prayer time. As soon as she dismissed us, we were to find a corner of camp and complete the devotional in our workbook together.

"Where do you want to go, sweetie?" Momma asked as we poured out of the chapel basement, like humidity that had been pent up too long. I shrugged. I didn't think I could look her in the eye. Hours ago, I would have sneakily arranged for us to sit in earshot of the Bullmans so that Lois could hear my superior devotional skills. But now I was sure God had rendered me unable to devote much of anything. The missions T-shirt on my back was feeling more and more like a yoke.

Momma said that if I didn't mind, she wanted to sit some-place cool, the heat was getting to her. We passed the pool area, where several pairs of moms and daughters had gathered, and where I overheard one momma saying, "Better not sit on the edge like that. It looks like the concrete is breaking off in places."

We decided to go back and sit in the van we'd come in.

"I don't know what to say, Em," Momma said, looking out the window to the mountains, through a fence that was torn in so many places it looked like a mangled fishnet stocking.

I don't know if it was just the sweat or real tears, but I felt the shame of the lie I'd told running down my face.

"Momma, I'm sorry about . . . the T-shirt, you take mine because . . ."

"Oh, Em, don't be silly. The truth is, I was relieved I wouldn't have to take that home and have to wear—" She caught herself. "Let's go ahead and get going on that devotional, why don't we?"

"You were *what*?"

Momma closed her eyes. She'd forgotten that her role as Blameless Confidante didn't apply in front of her own children. We were the one exception.

"I didn't mean . . . I didn't mean to say anything disparaging about the GA camp. I mean, these women try hard, real hard. It's just that . . . Since the time I remember coming, since the time Aunt Kit and your Mimi came, it's different. Things have changed. The Baptist Girls Club has changed. It's harder to know if you want to wear their T-shirts and their pins anymore."

The air inside the van seemed to thin. I had never, *ever* heard my momma so much as hint that she didn't like her job, her role. It was plain to see that she lived in a world where whole camps were created so that women could become what she was, by family—married to the Word. Her home was a model with a steeple everyone could see but her. Her children rose up and called her blessed, wearing halos that everyone could see but her. And she herself wore an invisible, permanent tiara, a beacon and an ever-shining guide that everyone paid homage to but her.

"What do you think is bad about it?"

"Oh, I don't think it's bad," she said. "I just think us girls have outgrown it, is all. All this. Little Miss Baptist camps; brochures that act like the modern girl's greatest thrill in life is to go way off in the middle of nowhere, only to sit in the grass and make pot holders. We can serve now in ways that go beyond Sunday coffee, but no one's noticed it. Our voices have gotten louder. No wonder the cabin walls are cracked. No wonder the pool is cracked and overflowing. But nobody's fixed poor Mary Jane's microphone. Now that, my daughter, is a shame."

Momma and I sat in silence for a minute as clouds drifted across power lines that were trying, in vain, to tow Redemption Gap into the new century. A cracking PA system announced that we had ten minutes to complete our devotionals. I opened the pink workbook and read aloud to Momma:

"We are in the woods at Redemption Gap. People often associate the woods with darkness, and with monsters that are hiding and waiting to strike. Sin is like that. It hides in the corners of our lives, ready to come out when we aren't paying attention. What is your monster? What is the thing that you will pledge to work hard to fight off during your time with us at camp?"

Momma gave me a teacher look—eyebrows raised, ready to catch my response. I spoke as solemnly as I could.

"The monster I will try to fight is . . . the Ministration."

My mother shrieked so hard with laughter that I was sure someone outside had heard her.

"I do believe mother–daughter bonding is achieved!" she said. "Can we go home, now?"

"No, Mother, we have to do good by Daddy and stay," I laughed.

"Well, he owes us."

Later that night, as I lay in my bunk above Momma, listening faintly for the Ministration creeping near in the woods (I should be so lucky), I thought about what she'd said, about Redemption Gap being sad, tired. I knew in my heart that there had been a time in recent memory—maybe a year ago, maybe just a few months—when I would have thought this place was beautiful. My cabin would have been a roadside mansion set aside by God for the training of his most select servants; my bunk, an apostle's throne. I would have looked at Mary Jane Armbruster, whose very picture was featured in nearly every GA guidebook I'd ever owned, and I would have had to hold myself back from asking for autographs.

But now, the Acteen crown was looking more like paste and dented foil in the pure, baptizing light of the mountains. So were her seekers. It made me wonder what daybreak might reveal, and whether all the trophies of grace I'd spent polishing in the case of my soul, for a lifetime, weren't slowly losing their shine.

But this wasn't what stuck in my head as I fell asleep. No, out of all the ragged mountain shadows, the pale ghosts of weakened women that had cast their weary pall over the "most exciting trip of my preteenage lifetime," one moment still glowed like a campfire in the wilderness. It was my momma's smile, lit from the front with sunlight reflected off the cracked van dashboard. At the end of the day, it was all I needed to love the trip, to love the church camp. There may not have been much in Redemption Gap, but there was joy for Emy Hancock seeping through the empty hollers. Maybe that was where it always lived, I thought. Maybe joy was what you had when they took everything else away from you. Or tried to. It wasn't in clean pools or uncracked tennis courts. It was being alone in the car with your mother's laugh, and nothing else but the sunset.

Lesson 8

Mimi and Meg

Peace

THE WRETCHED IMMORTAL

There was one bit of Baptist doctrine that I never could swallow, even as a little child. The feeding of five thousand from one fish, I believed. That my father could stop hellfires in a single dunk, I believed. But there was one part that my soul never accepted. That was the part about the prize we got at the end of the believing.

Heaven. Eternity. Forever. Never dying. *Forever.*

My problem was not with any of these things existing. My problem was with the fact that they were supposed to be rewards.

From the year I finished preschool to the year I entered middle school, I spent two Sunday afternoons a month making a pilgrimage that was as packed with spirituality as any morning service. Stopping once at Kentucky Fried Chicken so that our souls could be refreshed, the Hancock family made its way to the Damascus Long-Term Care Hospital (though, to all who lived there, the place was nicknamed "Heaven's Waiting Room").

On the last of these Sundays, as on all the others before it, my run up the wheelchair ramp with Meg made me dread that I had gone too heavy on the coleslaw. My stomach was not yet spiritually mature enough to avoid jumping at the sight of what it was about to encounter.

Inside the glass double doors was a true land of miracles. It was bright white and silver and gleaming, as if it might blow out any unworthy, dirty child with a single burst of fluorescent light. Here and there, blind men saw—or at least they seemed to, as they shouted out to Meg and me from their wheelchairs, lined up along the corridors. Others called out from their beds in tongues. One woman in particular, a big fat lady named Alma who, a nurse told us, had been there since she was nine years old, always caused a terrible uproar and had to be restrained whenever she saw Meg and me walk past her room.

This day was no different. Alma screamed as we rounded the corner, and I shrank up next to Momma, though I tried my best to fight the urge. I always felt horrible guilt when I did not have instant, holy love for one of God's fellow children. Though today, something else rooted me to the spot as well—the fear of the impending, dreadfully ethereal quiet that awaited us a few feet away in my grandma Mimi's room. There, eternity had seeped in with the anesthetics that dulled all things, and the hours slowed in time to the intermittent beats of electric monitors. There was no movement, no excitement, not even the rush of fear from some random outburst. Adults called the place "peaceful." I knew it as the home of a dreaded stillness that did not promise to go away. Once inside, even the ragged music of the gospel radio station that crackled over the PA system seemed like magnificent relief.

Mimi was just as we had left her the last time—wearing the pale pink nightgown Momma had given her for Christmas; eyes, barely blinking, staring at the ceiling; hands tightly gripping little towels, the way they had ever since the operation day when she fell asleep. She would be this way forever, a grandmother I had never seen. The one I knew had bright red curls and a purse that could snap open and closed, like an alligator's mouth. She was laughing, always laughing, in the parking lot of Hearst's Department Store, where she and Momma and Aunt Kit had been asked to "kindly keep control of their children or remove them," after Clayton had reached from his stroller and stuck a purple lollipop to a mannequin's skirt.

This new person, whom everyone called Mimi, could not laugh. Could not eat or drink or sing the funny song about the peanut on the railroad track. She was at peace. Too alive for heaven; too dead for our world. Just how she'd ended up that way was, by that time, up to the Kentucky Court of Appeals to decide. All I knew was that she'd been celebrating at my birthday party one day, her last hurrah before a simple surgery to check and make sure she'd beaten all the colon cancer that had slowed her down (but only a little) the year before. Two hours later she was asleep, forever. What happened in between I'd scraped together from eavesdropping sessions Suzanne and I conducted when our mommas and Grandpa D gathered around the coffee table with the lawyer and talked in low tones about "the case."

Sometime in the moments after she came out of surgery, something went wrong with Mimi's heart—an attack, a stroke, no one was really sure. What was certain is that no one came to help her until a patient in the next bed called the nurse's station to say that Mimi's lips were blue. By then, it was too late to wake up my grandmother. Somehow, while no one was listening, she'd fallen into the crack that all things baptism and Bible forgot to cover.

Six months before that last Sunday-afternoon visit, my family stood in front of the Circuit Court of Briggs County, with some of the congregation of Damascus Baptist, my mother's home church, gawking in the pews behind us, gasping as we took the position, for the first time in our lives, that the passing of a life wasn't really God's will after all. The court, high on its pulpit, in a tone my father could never hope to achieve on his most judgmental holy day, said we were wrong. The people of Damascus Baptist said Amen, and left my mother alone at the great altar of laws, scathing whispers their only benediction.

Only one person never seemed overly depressed by what was happening with Mimi. Mimi's second husband (her first had passed away long before I was born), the man we called Grandpa D, doted and spoke and sang hymns to my grandmother all day, every day, just as if they'd never left their porch swing. He was, Daddy said, "a true man of faith." It was a title I'd never heard my father bestow on anyone before; it was almost as if he was acknowledging that some lay grandfather out there was closer to God than he was. Because he hadn't entered our family until he and Mimi married, when I was about four years old, I never felt like I "knew" Grandpa D; not the way I knew Grandy, Daddy's father. And what I did know made me wonder if he was a real man or something out of a parable—a figure that someone created because they meant him to inspire reverence in you, but who in reality just inspired such unreal, fearsome strangeness that you didn't want to get too close to him in case you were irradiated with a lethal amount of holy goodness.

I knew that Grandpa D knew intensive care units well. His first wife, whom he married young, had died in an accident. The second, with whom he had several children, passed away from a fast-moving form of cancer. And then there was Mimi, and the awful day that eternity interfered in his marriage and invited her to its side. Grandpa D had cried, but he'd also kept on as if nothing was wrong with Mimi—bringing her new nightgowns, reading to her from the Bible, even keeping her breathing. About a year into Mimi's illness, Grandpa D had taken my grandmother, in a special chartered ambulance, to see a faith healer who was appearing at a Knoxville arena. Because Mimi's respirator couldn't be plugged in on the road, Grandpa D and a nurse had taken turns inflating my grandmother's lungs by hand, using an air bag, the entire six hours there and back.

Grandpa D just sat there smiling that last Sunday, while the same doctor came in, as he did every time, lifted each of Mimi's eyelids, and adjusted a tube here and there. The doctor spoke to Momma in the same words I had heard him repeat visit after visit—"comfortable" and "stable" and "no sign of change." Then he and Grandpa D left us alone for our Christian ceremony.

Momma called on my sister to do her part first, drawing her out from behind the bureau. She directed Meg to take one of Mimi's hands, and Meg balked about not wanting to touch the red-brown IV bruises that covered the fragile skin. But Momma's face fell and Meg obeyed. She followed the drill of telling Mimi about her week at school. As usual, neither Mimi nor Momma seemed to notice that Meg recounted the same week, right down to the weather and the stories read, every single time. Then Meg was released to the waiting room, where the same broken toys that had been there since the 1970s seemed to have found their own eternity.

I stood up straighter, knowing that my duty was next (and

feeling that I had to make an effort at looking nice, so as not to shake Momma's belief that her mother could see). The tube in Mimi's throat made a low gurgling sound, and I stared at it as I spoke to her, trying hard to believe that real words were somehow forming out of it and I just couldn't understand them. I nodded and laughed and tried to make conversation that would sustain Momma's hopeful glances, but near the end I felt dizzy—almost as if my words were personally filling Mimi's respirator with air. If I let down even for a moment, the family matriarch would die and take the rest of us with her.

Momma let me stop, and announced that we should go ahead and say our prayer before visiting hours were over. And I took her hand, and Daddy's hand across the bed, and Momma and Daddy each gripped one of Mimi's withered little claws. Then Daddy began. He asked God, in His infinite wisdom, to return Mimi to us. To take her from the Valley of the Shadow and bring her back into the light of day. The prayer was short and well practiced, tied up at the end with a solemn "Amen" and a quick "I'll bring the car around."

Momma nodded. She did not look away from her mother's face as Daddy left the room. Instead, she grabbed a hair pick from her purse and began combing the little rats out of the front of Mimi's hair. I just stood and stared, and wondered how often Mimi had done the same thing to Momma, while Momma fought her tooth and nail and begged to go back into the pool again. *This was it*, I thought. The burden of forever did not rest in the heavy brass cross that hung above Mimi's bed. It was wrapped up in something as tiny as a little comb. It did not sit, easy and golden, in some lofty place; it shook, in little trembling hands.

I wandered out into the hallway and rested against the

door frame while Momma fulfilled her tireless duty. She had tried to share the weight of Mimi's immortality with us, but it was to be shouldered by Mimi's child alone.

I was standing there, inhaling the dirty-bedpan smell that always seemed to usher us back out into the world, when I heard that Momma was not ready to leave. She spoke in low tones, hoping that the hum of Mimi's machines would drown her out. But her voice was too strong, more calm and steady than I had ever heard in this place.

"Momma," she said. "Dear Momma. I'm only going to be able to say this once, so I hope to the dear Lord that you are in a place where you can hear me. Everything you just heard Greg say . . . well, I love him and he loves you and he means nothing but the best. But I am here to tell you that I absolutely do not want you coming back into this world, if it's too hard for you. Do you hear me?"

Her voice cracked, and I heard it trail off into tears that she quickly rescued with laughter, as she always did, and as I always would.

". . . God, Momma, I sound just like you! Can you believe it? That just goes to show you, there's plenty of our stubborn blood left in this earth even without you, so don't hold on on account of that!"

She paused. Three slow beeps of the monitor.

"No, I mean that. If you need to go, you go. I'll be fine. The girls are great, and they will be wonderful, and we will all see you someday. But you don't have to stay here and wait it out with us, if it hurts too badly. I want you to know that. Okay, go on now, Momma. I love you, but please go on."

That night, with no warning and "no noticeable change"

according to the doctor, Mimi passed away. Momma's cries were louder and more filled with hurt than I had ever heard them. Daddy told Meg and me to go back to bed after the phone call from Grandpa D came in, but we stayed in the hallway. We listened to our mother, who was trying to refuse us as much of her own pain as possible, though she knew and we knew it would be our task to receive all of it someday. She cried into Daddy's ever-absorbent bathrobe, moaning about how it had been all her fault, how she had told her own mother to turn away from a life that might have lasted a lot longer.

Daddy held her, and told her that it was in God's hands, and that God had probably been waiting for Momma to say good-bye. That part of His gift of eternity to us was the right to give it up to Him, when we wanted. But we had to want to, first.

TRESPASSERS WILL BE BAPTIZED

AND THE ANGELS SANG

Mimi was laid to rest on an overcast Saturday afternoon. Afterward, Momma and I leaned against the front of the station wagon, out in front of Gardenia Bakery. The smell of rolls filled up the empty sidewalks.

It was quiet. Damascus was always quiet, but this was different. There were whispers underneath the silence. I wondered if Momma could hear them as she stood there, limp against the bumper, gazing at the outline of the old Hearst's Department Store, where Mimi had helped her try on every prom dress she'd ever bought. A sign in the window scheduled the store's permanent closing.

"Goodness is supposed to live forever," she breathed, so softly I could hardly hear it.

I didn't know what to say, and didn't want to say anything. To come up with any comfort, I'd have to first think about what it would be like to try to have faith in a world without a momma. I didn't know if such a thing was possible. It seemed ungodly.

Part of me was desperate to fill the silence, though. Part of me was scared that if I didn't, the echoes of what I'd heard that morning would grow so loud in my brain that my mother would hear them.

"You know what Lolly Jenkins said she heard, back when

she was volunteering down at Damascus Long-Term Care . . . ," a lady with a scratchy voice had said as I washed my hands in the bathroom of Damascus Baptist, after the funeral.

". . . said Greg and Sharon thought about *pulling the plug*. Can you imagine? He's a *preacher*, and this church raised her and . . . good Lord, I can't even think about it."

"Heaven help them," said someone else.

"Heaven help them," said another someone else.

"And this business about how they sued the hospital, that's just tacky. Somebody there might have made a mistake, sure. People just make mistakes. But I believe that when something like this happens, it's the will of God, and they just need to accept it."

"Yes, yes. Why on earth do people just refuse to accept it, why on earth?"

"Why, half this town works at that hospital! Sharon's and Kit's own kids was born there! And this is how they behave. High-and-mighty talk coming from a girl who Lolly says actually *prayed* that her mother would *die*, sometimes. You hear that? A minister's wife!"

"Heaven help them, I know, I know . . ."

"Well, if anything good comes out of poor Sylvia dying, I hope that her kids get taught that they aren't God. There, I've said it. I've said it and I'm going to pray for it, and I think I'll put it on the list so that this whole church—the church that raised those girls—prays for it, too."

"Amen, amen."

I searched my mind quickly for anything—anything—I could say that might drown out the Damascus Angels' murmuring in my head. But all I could think to say was—

"What . . . what are you looking at, Momma?"

"Just Kappel's jewelry store," she whispered, not blinking. "You see it? That marquee has been there since before I was born. They engraved my baby spoon and my class ring. They sat behind us at Damascus Baptist. And last month, Mr. Kappel sat on the back row of Mimi's jury. He slept through almost half the trial."

Momma's voice was calm, but I noticed that her hands were shaking, gripping the straps of her purse, tighter and tighter . . .

"And over there, see? That's where my daddy's newspaper was. He ran that paper for a decade at a loss, because he thought this little dent-in-the-road deserved a paper as much as anybody else. Nobody ever said thank you; he just kept doing it. Printed all the church materials, too, for free. Bet you didn't know that. Nobody knew that."

We stood there for what seemed like a long time, till a leaf drifted across the empty street. There hadn't been a single car pass the whole time. We were alone in Momma's town full of angels.

"It's so still" was all I could think of to say.

"Everyone's in church," Momma said.

"But it's Saturday, Momma."

"Everyone's still in church."

Lesson 9

Sunday morning service

Self-Control

CAT'S IN THE MANGER

It wasn't until the evening after we buried Mimi that I truly understood what Daddy had meant, all the times he'd preached that the faithful could "move heaven and earth." The Damascus Road we drove out of town on that night wasn't the same one that had burned itself a map behind my eyelids, summer after hot Bluegrass summer, singed at the corners with cookout smoke, scrawled over at every curve with the drawls of locals, shouting and waving from their front yards and never failing to recognize Momma and Aunt Kit, even through the dust.

This road was different. It seemed narrower; straighter. While we were in the funeral home, the Damascans seemed to have teamed together to change the landscape. The fireflies were gone and the grass was still. All the swinging front porch screens were noiseless and shut, and the air was more cool and crisp than I'd ever felt it.

"Hmmm . . . ," Momma moaned from the backseat, where she'd slept for the past hour. "That's Edna Mayfield, my high school gym teacher, watering those rhododendrons."

"Oh!" I chimed in, relieved that my mother had stirred at all. She'd fought for so long—helping, praying, hoping; holding my grandmother's head above water with all her strength—that part of me was surprised she hadn't passed right along with Mimi, from sheer exhaustion. Just in case, I'd made a silent promise to God that I'd do everything I could to keep my own mother alive over the next few days. This would be the hardest time, Daddy said.

"Is Mrs. Mayfield the one, you know," I went on, "the one who made you those gym uniforms that—"

"Doesn't she know my momma is dead?" Momma interrupted. "Watering flowers like things are just business as usual. Doesn't she know, for God's sake?"

"Sharon, Dr. Baker left you a whole mess of those pills, if you need more," Daddy said. "The bag is under the seat."

Momma had gone back to dozing before he finished the sentence.

I had to say, whether under the influence of Valium or not, Momma did have a valid point. The whole drive, I'd been resting my feet on the stupid kiddie book the funeral home director had given Meg and me—*Why, Oh Why, Did Granny Die?* or something like that. She said she knew it was "just a *little* young for us, but we all had questions at times like this, didn't we?"

No, not unless we were deaf, blind, and retarded, I'd wanted to say. Lula Adams, proprietor of Adams Funeral Home, knew exactly why my grandmother had died. Why, oh why, did she know? Because *everyone* knew. Because Mimi had been passing away in the same place, in the same bed, on the same prayer request roll, for ten years. Her name was as routine a fixture at benefits, fund-raisers, and prayer meetings as blue Jell-O salad. And just like the ever-present salad at all those events, the issue of Mimi's condition was always acknowledged but seldom touched. Even by some of those who claimed to love

Jesus and love Mimi most deeply, and especially not after the lawsuit and the trial that divided Damascus.

We couldn't blame them, Daddy said. Some situations were so strange, so beyond human control, that even the best-intentioned Christians could not be expected to know how to act.

And we are? I'd snapped at him.

Yes, we are.

And that was that. It wasn't the first time I'd heard my father let all bad-behaving Christians off the hook on the "they just don't know what God wants them to do" excuse—the same one he didn't dare let slide with his own daughters. But it was the first time I got the feeling that even Daddy didn't believe it.

Yes, Mimi's situation was a new one to most in the great Baptist family of former congregants and friends we'd amassed across Kentucky. Mass deaths, they'd handled. New, unexpected lives, in the form of babies born to eleven-year-old girls in Appalachian missions projects, they'd handled. But an otherwise healthy, devout grandmother, whose soul had managed to land smack on the line between heaven and earth? Well, that was a new one. Were they supposed to rejoice, because Mimi didn't die on the operating table? Or weep, because she hadn't exactly survived, either? And what about her everlasting soul? Even after the most tragic of events, good Baptists could take comfort in the fact that at least the deceased's soul was up there on their side of the bleachers. But no one could account for the resting place of my grandmother's soul while she was comatose. Not even the most faithful among them could do it.

So when my family came knocking, seeking the same kinds of blessed reassurances we'd offered to homes in need since my father was ordained, those sweet, trying Christians had done the safest thing they knew to do—they shut their screen doors, turned their locks, and prayed. That was the one great fringe benefit of praying—no one dared disturb you as long as you were doing it. When all else failed, you could just choose to keep your eyes closed and your head bowed below the turmoil for all eternity.

Daddy couldn't really complain about that. He'd taught everyone he knew to do it. But something in his eyes that day—something new, simmering at the edges of the calm blue-gray that I'd never seen before—made me think that he wasn't satisfied with all their praying and eye shutting and milque-toast we-should-leave-it-in-God's-hands efforts. That day, the look I'd seen him flash at all the mourners at the funeral home, as they shook his hand and wept but wouldn't make eye contact, and that he now kept steady in the rearview mirror as the angels of Damascus, Kentucky, faded out of sight, was the same look that had always had the power to fill me with more guilt than two hours straight of damnation preaching. It was a sermon in a glance. And it said *I expected more from you.*

"Hmmm . . ." Momma stirred again. "The clock. We should have gone to get my clock . . ."

"We'll get it, sweetie," Dad said. "Please, try to rest. I'm sure Grandpa D will want to get together for Sunday dinner soon, and I can ask him to bring the clock then."

Even through her mumbling, we all understood what clock Momma was talking about right away. Actually, it didn't belong to her; her daddy had gotten it for Mimi as an anniversary present, shortly after my mother was born. It was just a small, carved mantel clock that had caught my grandfather's eye from the window of Hearst's Department Store, the day he had a new paycheck in his pocket. When the salesclerk told him the maker had named the clock "Sharon," the same name as his new baby daughter, Pap was sold.

For most kids, one parent's gift to another wouldn't have meant much. It would have just faded into the background of the chimney or corner cupboard, drawing eyes and sighs only when it had to be dusted as punishment. But the Sharon clock was the exception, because as far back as I could recall, most of my mother's family had lived up on the mantelpiece with it. The Campbells of Damascus—the "newspaper family," more than one old Damascus church lady had described them to me—were seldom front-page news themselves, but through Pap's headlines they gave the precious gift of highfalutin prominence to people who would never set foot beyond the town limits in their lives. I used to spend afternoons on my toes in front of Mimi's mantel, scrutinizing them, wondering how the whole history of a little town—every birthday, every anniversary, every first-bass-of-the-season-caught—could fit inside those heads and bodies that were so tiny, like my momma's. I wondered how those laughing eyes and wide grins, so electric, so glinting in the flashing pendulum of the clock that they seemed to be alive again, could have been snuffed out so early, and almost all by something as fleeting as a little tobacco smoke.

They were all warned, Momma would say, dusting each frame one at a time with the corner of her shirt. *Especially my daddy. He knew how all their lungs were. But he was stubborn.*

Then she'd replace each frame on the mantel—carefully, like it was the most fragile of babies—and sit still in front of the fire and doze to the ticking of the clock. It was the same sound her father had tuned his watch by, that her mother had used to gauge the arrival of company on Friday nights. It never died.

Even now, atop the fireplace in the house that Grandpa D was returning to alone, its toll would greet him. I'd heard him say, before, that the sound kept him awake at night, even back in his bedroom. But as long as Mimi was with him, he never stopped the pendulum. I wondered if he would now.

"Dad, watch out!"

The wheels of our station wagon squealed into the dust, roughly four feet into the last intersection in Briggs County. Of course, there were no other cars near the crossing. Momma mumbled something about the clock again, and Meg gave an indifferent sort of snort but didn't wake up. Her cure for deep grief and funerals was the same as it was for a bad dinner, or for a boring playmate she wished would leave the house. Sleep it off. Just sleep it off and it will go away. Her convenient slumber skills had frustrated me for a long time, but not lately, and especially not after seeing all the conveniently bowed heads at Mimi's funeral. Meg slept for the same reason most people prayed—just close your eyes long enough and hard enough, and someone else will take care of it.

"Oh, sorry, Miss Em," Daddy said. "I guess I've just been thinking a little too much."

I'd noticed. Daddy's eyes had barely left the rearview mirror, which was fixed on Momma and not on the road, since we'd crossed the Damascus Cemetery gates. I hadn't reminded him to concentrate until this point because, to tell the truth, I was afraid to. This was a different Daddy. The father I knew was a rock at sad events, especially where church people were concerned. He could work a pulpit and a wailing crowd like a NASA shuttle pilot, pulling a craft and Christian America's hopes out of a suborbital barrel roll, never breaking a sweat, and give all credit to the great Man at the control tower.

But not today. Today, I thought, he looked more like a man whose burden box had finally reached its limit. Whose soul, miraculous as it was, might just be ready to say, *No more.*

I pushed the thought from my mind as soon as it had entered. The very idea that my father might be struggling seemed as blasphemous as it was scary.

I wished I'd been the only one who'd entertained it.

"Miss Em, you awake?" Daddy finally said. Damascus was only about an hour behind us, but the drive seemed to have taken much longer.

"Yes, Dad. You know I can't sleep in the car."

"That's right, that's right." Daddy laughed, as if this piece of knowledge had just occurred to him. As if he hadn't had to pull over for me to be sick by the side of the highway every time my head had so much as drooped during a family vacation. Something was definitely not right.

"Well, so long as you're awake, so long as we've got some time here to talk, I thought I'd tell you."

Daddy looked at the dash and mumbled something about needing gas in a few miles. I relaxed a little. Whatever he was about to tell me couldn't have been too serious, if he was perfectly comfortable mixing auto maintenance talk right in with it.

"Miss Em, your momma and I have been talking for a while, and, well, I think it's time for me to stop. The pulpit, I mean. Preaching, the Convention, all of it. Time to move on to something new."

He said it as if he were remarking about switching brands of aftershave. But what I heard was more like an announcement that he was switching names, switching worlds, switching lives. Trading in what I'd always known, what I'd always taken pride in, for the type of "thing" that had always sounded with demonic undertones in every good old Baptist place I'd ever visited—something "new."

I couldn't do anything but swallow back a lump and nod out the window, at first. I did not know what to say to my father, and I knew that certain ideas coming to mind at the moment weren't the right ones.

A Preacher's Kid suddenly not being a Preacher's Kid anymore? Lots of PKs I knew would have absolutely wept for joy at the mere suggestion. No more Friday-night choir practices. No more of your dad being late for your birthday party because some geezer you'd never heard of came down with an enlarged prostate and requested a bedside prayer. No more perfect behavior; no more shunning the tight-jeans department at JCPenney. No more of God, and Dad, being in charge of everything and everybody, and being sung to and prayed to and revered by everything and everybody.

The thought wasn't as comforting as I'd hoped. Instead of sensing freedom in Dad's announcement, all I could feel was something like a horrible severing; a sharp cut away from everything I'd ever known. My mind flashed back to Mrs. Turner's classroom, and the guidance counselor coming in to tell us all one day that sometimes mommies and daddies made decisions to end their relationships, and that wasn't our fault at all, no sir. At the time, I'd thought of raising my hand and asking her whether she knew divorce was an abomination unto

God, as I'd heard said by one of the women in the prayer group Mrs. Turner herself attended. Instead I'd just kept my head low and colored. Divorce wasn't relevant to me or my family. Sin wasn't relevant to me or my family. Everyone knew that. Daddy of all people knew that.

Then why, as I watched the bluegrass drift by, country churches pressing us over their horizons one by one, as if striking my family from their mailing lists already, could I only picture that guidance counselor, reflected over my shoulder in the window?

Don't take it personally, dear, she said. *Just because your father doesn't love and adore Jesus Christ our Lord, Savior, and Reason for Being anymore, doesn't mean he doesn't love you!*

"You're upset," Dad said. "I knew it. Mom said . . ."

"No, no. I just . . ."

I said a silent prayer for guidance, for anything that would bring my father's sanity back and change his mind. I wasn't sure if it would work (after all, maybe my direct hotline had already been turned off), but then, a blessing of pure genius struck my troubled mind—

"I'm not worried about *me* . . . that would just, that would be selfish. But what about all those people out there who need you? What about all those people you promised to help? Who are waiting for you?"

At first, it seemed this might work. Dad rubbed his chin and seemed to be thinking. But then his voice dropped into an all-too-familiar register. The Sermon Voice. He hadn't lost it yet. And he'd already prepared this one, illustration-first.

"Miss Em, I don't know if you'd even remember this, but when you were real tiny and you lived in Stanton . . ."

"Dad . . ."

"Just hear me out. When we lived in Stanton, you found a cat out in front of the house one day. You named it Petunia, and . . ."

This was too much. I already knew what was coming. Dad had just ripped his daughter's identity to shreds; the least he could do was offer me some new material as consolation.

"I know, I know, I know this one, Dad. I wanted the cat as a pet, but you and Mom and God wanted it to have a place where it could play, and we didn't have a big enough house or yard. So you gave it away to another little girl, who was poor but had a big yard, plus nice normal parents who didn't do things like give her pets away in the name of the Lord. And the moral of this story is, sometimes we have to give souls away to other people, to other preachers, where they'll be better off, even though you'd love nothing more than to be their preacher and lead their houses for all eternity . . ."

Dad's eyes started to furrow. He was hurt, I could tell. But I didn't stop. I wanted him to feel his decision in the stomach, the way that I did. I kept going.

". . . and I was little and so I forgave, because that was all I knew how to do. That's all I've ever really known how to do. And that was fine, because I didn't have to do it that often. Most people never tried to hurt me in the first place, just because I was your daughter. But now . . ."

Dad reached out and touched my shoulder. I tried to move, but I couldn't cram myself any farther into the passenger's-side door.

"You want to stop? There's a Dairy Queen up ahead. I bet you and Meg would like some ice cream."

I didn't say anything. Daddy pulled in to the DQ anyway

but didn't get out of the car. We just sat there, parked at the edge of the lot, where a line of Dumpsters threatened to spill onto a picturesque patch of horse farm.

"Progress, progress," Dad whispered, shaking his head. After a while, he spoke again. He'd dropped the sermon tone.

"Well, if you'll let me finish now. Keep in mind that I'm only telling you this because your mother is passed out. Otherwise she'd have my hide for doing it without her."

I thought I heard Meg stir in the back. She might have been faking sleep by this point.

"... But that cat you found, Petunia? Honey, we didn't give it away to anyone. That was what we decided to tell you because you were too young to understand. We made up a story to let you think you'd done a good deed, and left it at that. You'd be surprised how many people that works with ..."

"Dad, you're not a preacher anymore. You said it, not me. That means it should now take you less than an hour to make a point."

"Yes, yes, anyway. The cat. You were barely toddling, out in the front yard with your momma planting flowers. Before she noticed, you'd wandered into a little culvert next to our driveway and picked up that stray kitten. I was working in the garage, and you brought it to me. You said 'Fix, Daddy.' I thought you meant some sort of a stuffed toy, but when I looked down, I saw that it was a real kitten, and it was badly hurt. Either a car had hit it or some animal had attacked it, and blood was all over your little hands."

"Gross! I don't remember any of that."

"Well, you wouldn't. My theory is that children who grow up around lots of saving never remember how hard and how messy things were before the saving, the baptism, and the cleaning and the healing actually happened. You just remember the good, after."

I stared at my hands, picturing the blood. I wondered if Dad was bluffing, if I really could have forgotten something like that. If I'd really been as naive to the messy side of everything he did. After all, I'd always considered myself such a spiritually aware, deeply in-touch soul, even in the Sunday School nursery department.

"So what did you do?" I asked.

"Took you to the doctor and had you checked for rabies, of course. Took the cat to the vet, too, had it put down. You were too little to understand that, though. All you really knew, all you really had confidence in, was 'Daddy, fix.' You said it with all the faith in the world."

I heard my father's voice crack. But he swallowed back whatever had threatened to emerge, like a good preacher. I supposed the ordination didn't wash out so easily, not even with the great baptizer of new ambition.

"So that's why you want to leave? Do you feel like you've been lying to people?" I asked. I sensed both Mom and Meg were awake in the back now. They had been for a while, but they weren't talking.

"No, it's not that. What it is is twenty years of a hundred and twenty people a day coming to your door, without a reservation in the world, saying 'Daddy, fix.' And you want to, you really do. You always try. But eventually you get tired. And eventually, you decide it's time to devote more energy to fixing things in your own house. Time to put yourself in the driver's seat, if only a little bit more. Things change, you know."

He looked at Mom in the rearview, and she gave just the slightest smile. And then my father looked at me. Without even turning my head, I could tell—at the center of that look was a prayer. *Please understand, Little Lamb. Please don't ask more things that I can't answer. Please let me go on and grow, because I am letting you.*

I had a snappy response planned that would smack him right in the soul. *What about the call? What about all the people Jesus ordered you to help? What about Meg and me, the ones who've grown up with the "preachers' kids have problems" hisses in the backs of the classrooms? Just what kind of stereotypes might be in store for ex-preachers' kids, huh? Would I step out into that dangerous territory my Sunday School teachers called "looking for direction," with all the other pathetic wanderers who bought crystal necklaces and New Age calming music and other ungodly things that made your muscles relax when God hadn't given them permission to do so? And what about poor Meg? Would she start piercing her eyebrows all over, like Jim and Tammy Faye's son after his daddy left the fold?*

But all I could do was stare out the window, at a house right next to a church at the county's edge. It was a parsonage, and the light was on. Somewhere inside, I thought of a little daughter who was picking out her dress for church the next day, hanging it on her closet door with reverence, like the holiest of garments, like something befitting the Crown Princess of White Oak Baptist as she went to appear before her father. Soon she'd say her prayers, and dream of the morning and of walking down the center aisle with her momma and sister; of the organ blaring a fanfare and sunlight pouring in pane-by-pane through the stained glass, like a thousand flashbulbs going off at once. And she'd feel the glamour and glory of believing, so strong that it kept her awake.

I thought of her, and of my own first pair of white patent-leather Sunday shoes, somewhere in the back of the closet, the shine long gone. And all I could say to my daddy was, "I just don't want it to end."

The truth was, though, I knew that it had been over for a while. Just what was "ending," I couldn't exactly say, but I'd felt it. Maybe it was because I was getting older. Maybe it was because Daddy was getting older. Either way, something had changed. Ever since I was born, church was the place of my fairy tales and fantasies; where handsome young deacons in tweed blazers talked with sparkling eyes about making miracles happen; where every family from the neighborhood was united as one on the same pew, if only for a morning; where old Aunt Vaney and her cronies held the status of regal matriarchs; and where a pair of used Guess jeans could grant me a holy power beyond measure.

But now, now as I'd seen more of the church and its people for what they were, as I'd come to understand more about the holy palace I'd once coveted so dearly, the magic seemed to be fading.

It was normal, Daddy said, as we finished those last miles toward home. The Holy Book was full of endings—deaths and resurrections, old testaments that had to pass away before the new could come. And the new was always better, wiser. But first you had to be willing to trespass away from the old, and baptize yourself in fresh waters. Daddy said that up until now, he'd always been the one who led us to the new places, the one who held our noses and did the dunking while all the turmoil of transition overhead passed. Now it was going to have to be our turn, and our choice—to see faith for what it was and love it anyway, or to go on, try nonbelieving for a while, and see how it fit. Every good Christian came to this crossroads, he said. Even the best of them. Especially the best of them.

And that was the end, Amen. It was the last sermon my father preached to me as a man fully ordained in the Baptist ministry.

It was also the last day Grandpa D would ever contact us. We never really talked about him or why he was gone. That half of our family, where so much had been torn in hurt, just sort of faded to a stop, like all Grandpa D's Christmas and birthday cards. It was to be expected, Daddy said. We had to leave the dead to bury their own dead. Grandpa D might have seemed supernatural to us, but he wasn't. He had to grieve in his own time, and we had to have faith that he'd come back to us. *He will*, Daddy said, *he will*.

After all, everyone always had. It was the Eleventh Commandment, my father often said, that you could never really get out of the shadow of the steeple you grew up under. People got mad at the church all the time. They swore at God. They shook their fists at my father. They wondered why things happened, what the "point of it all" was, and where the holy magic had ended. But eventually, something usually drew them back to their familiar place on the pew.

As I looked through the rearview mirror on the way home that night, I wondered what the "something" was. I looked at the road behind us, and I hoped it didn't lie beneath the earth back in Damascus, along with so much that my family had buried and left behind that day.

And I looked at the road ahead, and hoped that, if it was there, I'd find it. I'd keep on looking through the rain and dust, and I'd pray from then on with both eyes open.

Daddy and me

Benediction

One simple truth has guided all good Baptist children on faith journeys, ever since the Creation—you know a new beginning is happening because everything is dark. It doesn't last long, though. Jesus comes along eventually and leads you out of darkness, washes your windshield, shows you the clear path.

All I could think about on that freezing December night, as Meg and I drove along without a map, was that it was too bad Jesus didn't communicate with the streetlight operators of Damascus, Kentucky. Like many spot-in-the-road Bluegrass towns, Damascus called itself a "city built on faith." And it was a good thing—with hardly any streetlights or stoplights, house numbers few and far between, and cow pastures so close to the roads that the barbed wire threatened to scrape your paint job, you basically had to pray your way through town after dark.

"Wait, turn here! That's it! I remember the long driveway. That's definitely it," Meg shouted, adding that it was lucky her rear end had memorized every bump in the dirt road long ago or we'd have been lost for sure.

I pulled alongside the mailbox, where a brass plaque on the front was heavily rusted but still legible: DAVIDSON. Grandpa D's house.

"You're right. This is it."

And even in the dark, I could feel that it was. Every child's soul seeks out soft places to fall, early on. And the softest of these was always a grandmother's house, even if she wasn't there to greet you at the door anymore.

"Should we go in?" Meg asked.

"Just a minute. Just one minute."

The swift beating of my heart caught me suddenly off guard. I had expected this to be the easy part. The phone call was supposed to be the hardest part, and even it had gone better than I'd expected.

Though I knew the phone number would still be in my father's datebook, right up front on the "family" page, I still asked him where I could find it. Deep down, I was hoping Daddy'd volunteer to call Grandpa D for me. Or maybe talk me out of it.

But instead he just said, "You're sure you want to do this? I don't know what you'll get when you call, Em. I wish I could tell you."

I just nodded, but I'd never been so unsure of anything. There was a time in my life when Grandpa D had been the closest thing I'd ever seen to a living, breathing biblical figure. Not like a televangelist (or even a regular preacher like Daddy), who talked lots about all things holy. No, Grandpa D seemed to be possessed of a faith from a different time. He was larger—taller—than life, for starters, and had the snowiest snow-white hair I'd ever seen; a little like Charlton Heston with an east Kentucky accent. But you'd only hear that when he talked, which wasn't often. Most of our afternoons with him, when we weren't at Mimi's bedside, were spent under the willow tree in his yard, where he read his Bible in the shade; or at his pool, where Meg and I would practice our baptisms on our cousins and make him assign us scores.

That'n's a ten. Yep, that one took for sure.

A few times, I wandered to the pool edge, the question I wanted to ask so badly right on the edge of my lips:

How do you do it, sitting there so calm in that lawn chair where your second wife used to sit, before she died? Reading with a smile on your face, with the handmade bookmark Mimi made, while she could still embroider? Grandpa D, what exactly did they baptize you in? Molten steel? Did it hurt? And how did you do it without a daddy whose job it was to keep polishing your soul, to keep reinforcing it when you couldn't?

Neither my sister nor my cousins seemed to share the same fascination with their step-grandfather as I did. Suzanne always laughed at the stack of Gideon Bibles he kept inside the front door, ready to hand out to any Jehovah's Witness or Avon lady who might stop by. (Even my ordained father didn't do something that weird, she said.) And after Mimi died, Grandpa D seemed to fade from everyone's memory almost instantly. That is, except for Dottie Jane's. She kept a running tab of the dollar amounts he owed her in missed birthday and Christmas checks.

"Just forget it, Dot," Suzanne would say. "It's not like he was our real grandpa anyway."

The words always gave me a shiver. I had sometimes wondered whether Grandpa D was real at all. His presence had kept my grandmother breathing a decade longer than medical science had said she should. Part of me wondered if, the day she died, like some dramatic "true story" I'd heard told by a youth pastor, they would find no trace of Grandpa D on earth anymore. Maybe just a feather and a Bible on the edge of Mimi's open hospital room window. And when we asked the nurses where he'd gone, they'd say, *Who? There was never any man in here visiting her, not ever . . .*

"Em? Are you ready now?"

Meg was waving a hand in front of my face.

"Oh . . . yeah, I guess we'd better." Meg and I both took as long as we could putting our scarves and gloves back on, then we started the long trek down the driveway.

"I still can't believe you actually talked to him. That must have been weird."

"Well, it was at first, but then, I don't know, it was easy. It was like I'd just been talking to him the week before, you know?"

That wasn't exactly true, but it seemed like the right thing to say. The call hadn't gone badly, after all. I'd planned on my first attempt being a trial run, just to make sure I could muster the courage, so I called on a Sunday right after church. I was sure Grandpa D would still be in service, or at least not home quite yet. But he picked up the phone on the first ring.

I went through the embarrassing process of reintroducing myself to my own grandfather, so quickly that he had to ask me to stop and start over. There was a long pause when I was finished, but then . . .

Oh yes . . . Sharon's daughter. Oh yes, of course. How are you?

It was a very polite beginning. Not a typical Hancock family beginning, where the how-the-heck-are-yous flowed so effusively through the line that they nearly knocked you on your back. But polite, and still very much in the realm of loving.

We talked for only a couple of minutes. I asked if he still had Momma's clock, by chance, and if he'd be willing to part with it. Meg and I wanted to surprise Momma with it at Christmas. I told him I didn't have much money but would be glad to pay him back over the next few months, if that would be okay. He said that wasn't necessary; he knew where the clock was and would be glad for me to have it back. Then the doorbell rang and he had to go. He was sorry we couldn't chat more, but there would be time enough for that when I came to pick up the clock, the next Saturday night at eight o'clock. I said I would bring my sister along with me, and maybe a few pictures. He said he'd like that.

And that was the end.

"Oh, no." Meg had stopped dead in her tracks. "Emy, look. At least Mimi didn't have to live to see that."

To my right, spotlighted with a lawn lamp, I saw exactly what Meg was talking about. If there was one thing Mimi had never liked about her fellow residents of Damascus, it was their affection for lawn statuary—forest animals, permanent manger scenes, all kinds of things. Now perched in her front yard was a five-foot, sculpted concrete basket, decked on the sides with squirrels. It was on top of the stump where her willow tree had once been.

The site was almost enough to make me cry, but instead I mumbled *shhhh* to Meg. What if the new Mrs. Davidson heard her? Daddy had already warned us that he didn't really know much about Grandpa D's life after Mimi, but he did know that he'd remarried. We were going to have to be respectful of that if we were even going to think about visiting him. I said that we would. But it was strange to think about Grandpa D's life going on without us, probably with new grandchildren. I wondered if they were the ones who'd made him cut down the willow.

When we got to the bottom of the front porch steps, I made Meg stop again. I just wanted to stand for a second, in the porch lights, looking at the door like I had so many times before, sometimes with arms full of birthday presents or cookies Momma and I had baked. The front door was the one part of the house that looked the same. And as much as I couldn't wait to get inside, couldn't wait to look into Grandpa D's eyes and finally ask him for the secret to his great faith—he, who had surely had every ministry a church could invent tossed, singing and clapping with laser lights, onto his doorstep, yet had still managed to rise above all the silliness and the doubts, to never take his eyes off some true star that so few could see. How I longed to have that kind of faith in the church, like I'd had as a little girl before my father, again. I knew I was going to have to open the door to get it.

But after two long rings of the bell, no one answered. Finally, Meg noticed an oversize shoe box, off to the side of the porch. Inside was my mother's clock. There was no note.

Meg put her hand over mine as we finished replacing the duct tape on the sides of the box, in silence.

"Maybe he forgot, Sis."

"No. No, the time was his idea. He didn't forget. The fact that he left the clock proves that he didn't forget."

"Well," Meg said. "It was probably an emergency, then. They probably ran out of Bibles at the Motel 6 or something."

"But no note? He knew we came all this way!" I felt new tears sting the corners of my eyes in the cold.

"I know. I guess he just wasn't ready yet after all."

My shorter, younger, more immature sister put her arm around me, and I felt again that pastoral touch she was born with, that her stuffed animals had always known. We headed back to the car.

Midway down the driveway, we stopped. Right at the same time, as if on command from something unseen. We looked at each other then turned to walk across the driveway and down the hill, where the edge of Grandpa D's floodlight proved that the swimming pool still stood.

The gate latch still stuck if you pulled on it too hard, but after a couple of tries we had it open.

"Wow." It was all Meg could say.

We didn't need to bother with the gate after all. On the far side of the pool, the fence had blown almost all the way down. A carpet of leaves, from who knew how many falls, blanketed everything. All the lawn chairs were strewn across the top of the cover, with the exception of one. Grandpa D's reading chair, his baptism judging chair, sat where it always had, next to the diving board. The seat had long since rotted out of it.

We stood there for a good while, ignoring the cold, pointing out the places where we'd played our games a long time ago, and where Momma and Mimi and Kit had once sunned themselves in a row. It was where we'd stood in the water, one of us holding our breath underneath, the other standing and reciting "rich man, poor man, beggar man, thief; doctor, lawyer, Indian chief." The point in the verse where you couldn't hold your breath anymore and had to rise to the surface was supposed to dictate what you became when you grew up. For a long while, each of us had shot for "lawyer." "Preacher" wasn't on the list. Maybe because it was a given.

Meg and I didn't notice the headlights behind us.

"Girls? Are you in there?"

I ran toward the gate, shouting Grandpa D's name like some five-year-old before I could stop myself. But even through the whipping of the wind, I could tell the voice didn't belong to him. Daddy stepped carefully into the floodlight and through the pool gate.

I started to explain the clock box and the events of the night, but the expression on my father's face told me I didn't have to.

"He wasn't home" was all I could get out, before Daddy pulled both Meg and me into his sides. We all stood there, looking at where the water had been, as if we might be able to make out a reflection of happier times in this place. Daddy said that he'd had a feeling this was going to happen, and that he wished he'd caught up to us before we had to go through it alone.

"But we didn't," I told him. To be sure, what I felt now was sadness. I was disappointed. I missed my grandfather. But never, the whole time, had I felt alone. I looked up the hill to Grandpa D's house, where I hadn't noticed until now that no Christmas lights or tree burned in the windows. The bumper sticker that had once hung from the mailbox, inviting any passers to come in and hear the Good News, was gone, too.

I looked at my father and sister, and I looked back up at that dark house. *That*, I knew now, was *alone*. Alone wasn't a house where family had died or left; it was a house where faith itself had been allowed to move away.

That moment, I realized the core sermon Daddy had been trying to give me all my life. Faith could be a ridiculous houseguest sometimes. It wore flamboyant T-shirts and gaudy promise rings, sometimes with shiny, white patent-leather shoes. It sang obnoxious songs. It talked about sex at inappropriate times. It was bossy and braggerty. It could be condescending and rude.

But once in a while, it could bring an entire warehouse full of turkeys back from the dead. It could give a pair of acid-washed blue jeans the wonder-working power. It could turn siblings into prophets; parents into healers. Even estranged step-grandparents into gods who walked on water. And no matter where you lived, and no matter what crazy forms it took in what unfamiliar towns, it was always better to just let it in than to shut it out, even when it didn't "feel" magical, even when it felt superficial, or as contrived and silly as the biggest Christmas Pageant Mrs. Mounts ever put on.

Faith's magic was usually subtle; so much so that you didn't notice it until you were in a place where it was gone, with nothing but the cold wind and your tears to baptize away the hurt.

"Better go, girls. We're trespassing," Daddy said. "I wish we could say this was still our sacred ground, but it ain't."

We headed back up the hill to our cars. By then, the night had grown so overcast that the streets were blacker than before; any starlight that might have guided us was completely gone. So I did what I always did. Meg sat asleep on the passenger's side, the still-constant ticking of Momma's clock lulling her away. And I followed my daddy's lights on the horizon, all the way back home.